ADVANCE PRAISE

'Everyone desires to be a good leader. Most of us believe that leadership attributes are abstract and developed mostly from learning, experience and circumstances. Dr Anjana Sen has delved into a new approach and rationale, based on neuroscience inputs. She conveys that Ultra Special Senses of the brain contribute much to the development, strengthening and prioritization of leadership attributes in a person.

Dr Sen explains attributes of a person in a practical, easy-to-understand dialogue with Tan Tan. Two examples are as follows:

- "The presence of hope engenders positive emotions such as courage and thus has a motivational impact on the performance of a person."
- "Self-worth is the belt which straps values safely in the driver's seat."

What's Your Superpower? Ultra Special Senses and You is a path-breaking narrative for better understanding and imbibing leadership traits and qualities. A self-help for aspiring leaders and those interested in this important subject.'

General Ved Prakash Malik, *PVSM, AVSM,*
Former Chief of Staff, Indian Army

'In today's world of flux, all of us are constantly juggling various aspects of our lives and wishing for balance. There are many books which are written with the aim of helping us to discover within ourselves how to tackle and deal with our varied emotions. Anjana Sen with her latest book *What's Your Superpower?* takes readers through a discovery of Ultra Special Senses, all of 15, within each of us to help deal with different situations in life. Since she is from a medical background and her interests include research around neurosciences, the same is reflected in her book to help us make connections. What helps to lighten the scientific aspects is the introduction of Tan Tan (illustrated by her) who is a reflection of the reader in situations we can relate to. The conversations between the author and Tan Tan make those parts endearing. Those interested in the connection of neurosciences and emotions will find plenty of it in this book.'

Bipasa Mukherjee, *Special Education Consultant,*
Anandniketan School, Ahmedabad, India,
and Chittagong, Bangladesh

'At the time when the youth is increasingly grappling with questions of identity, self-worth and the purpose of life, this book comes as a much-needed tool to help them find an enhanced sense of self and belongingness. This book will encourage its readers to delve more into their inner self and explore their thoughts and emotions. It will be a journey that would make you a more confident and resilient person!'

Dr Sanjay Chugh, *Senior Consultant Psychiatrist,*
New Delhi

'A brilliantly simplified text, detailing complex concepts of the subconscious and conscious states of mind at play in our development of self-worth, resilience and leadership qualities. With a firmly rooted background in neuroscience, the author gives very astute insights into our Ultra Special Senses and allows us to analyse ourselves very subtly. By the time we have absorbed one concept and applied it to ourselves, we notice ourselves smiling and turning the page.

A must-read book for those aspiring to be in leadership roles, and also those attempting to understand and influence human behaviour.

Dr Anjana Sen makes an extremely credible and intelligent effort to introduce us to wisdom, through understanding of concepts that govern our mind and influence social interactions. This book emerges as an understated, elegant, scientific guide to recognition and development of an ultra-special sensitivity towards fellow beings.

Advantage humanity!'

Dr Geeti Chadha, *Neurologist and Clinical Neurophysiologist, Mubarak Al-Kabeer Hospital, Kuwait University*

'Anjana straddles neuroscience and the psychology of wellness effortlessly, making this book an invaluable self-help guide for aspiring leaders. The easy conversational flow with Tan Tan enhances understanding of USSs with lots of insightful pointers to practise in daily life. For millennials struggling to cope with rejection, even relevance, in an increasingly digital world, the timing of *What's Your Superpower?* is indeed opportune.'

Jyotirmoy Bose, *Organization Transformation Therapist and Leadership Coach, Delhi NCR*

WHAT'S *your* SUPER-POWER?

Ultra Special Senses and You

ANJANA SEN

⑤SAGE | Response Business Books

Los Angeles | London | New Delhi
Singapore | Washington DC | Melbourne

First published in 2019 by

SAGE Publications India Pvt Ltd
B1/I-1 Mohan Cooperative Industrial Area
Mathura Road, New Delhi 110 044, India
www.sagepub.in

SAGE Publications Inc
2455 Teller Road
Thousand Oaks, California 91320, USA

SAGE Publications Ltd
1 Oliver's Yard, 55 City Road
London EC1Y 1SP, United Kingdom

SAGE Publications Asia-Pacific Pte Ltd
18 Cross Street #10-10/11/12
China Square Central
Singapore 048423

Published by Vivek Mehra for SAGE Publications India Pvt Ltd. Typeset in 11/14 pt Bembo by Fidus Design Pvt Ltd, Chandigarh.

Library of Congress Cataloging-in-Publication Data Available

ISBN: 978-93-532-8613-2 (PB)

SAGE Team: Manisha Mathews, Shruti Gupta and Rajinder Kaur

Dedicated to Generation Next!

Thank you for choosing a SAGE product!
If you have any comment, observation or feedback,
I would like to personally hear from you.

Please write to me at **contactceo@sagepub.in**

Vivek Mehra, Managing Director and CEO, SAGE India.

Bulk Sales

SAGE India offers special discounts
for purchase of books in bulk.
We also make available special imprints
and excerpts from our books on demand.

For orders and enquiries, write to us at

Marketing Department
SAGE Publications India Pvt Ltd
B1/I-1, Mohan Cooperative Industrial Area
Mathura Road, Post Bag 7
New Delhi 110044, India

E-mail us at **marketing@sagepub.in**

Subscribe to our mailing list
Write to **marketing@sagepub.in**

This book is also available as an e-book.

CONTENTS

PREFACE

As a medical student, I held the dream of qualifying to be a doctor to treat sick people and make them strong again. The adage 'Prevention is better than cure' turned up every now and then, though there was a complete subject named Preventive and Social Medicine, it appeared pale next to the rockstar discipline of internal medicine and the swathe of surgical specialties. The wisdom of the adage, though irrefutable, was eclipsed and prevention slipped low in the priorities of the curriculum. Through many years of professional life as a physician and ophthalmologist, experience of the real world seeped into the subconscious, a phenomenon I now regard as the 'growth of wisdom'. There was no time to connect with it, but wisdom lived incognito in my head and surprised me with an unexpected appearance. I was often invited to speak on a trending topic of general health. On one such occasion, I chose to speak on just health, and not disease.

Turning the spotlight on health changed my perspective. Health does not come from diet or supplements. It comes from peace and contentment. Peace does not come from doing nothing. It comes from finding courage to stand up for what we believe in. It comes from learning how to forgive and finding the fortitude to let things alone, and we need wisdom to know when and how to just let it be.

Reaching out to people to explain how their bodies react to stress resulted in more enduring results than prescribing medicines. I opted out of the practice of clinical medicine and took on the mantle of facilitator of workshops on emotional intelligence and neurophysiology of emotion, explaining the mechanism of balancing ego discomfort of criticism and the need for managing anger. Participants found the inputs applicable in both personal and professional spheres. Restoration of motivation and relationships resulted in soaring professional success. Improved relationships with the self, turned around personal lives and biochemical parameters reverted to healthy levels. The results prompted me to take on individual cases that required dedicated attention and customized coaching. My medical studies provided the foundation to continue exploring latest research in the area of neurology and physiology of emotions that provide the infrastructure for the development of competencies required to navigate reality.

Keeping my mission of 'Maximizing Potential and Minimizing Stress' in view, I wrote my first book *Get the Ego Advantage!* (in 2006) and some academic papers on the topic of emotional intelligence and applicable neuroscientific insights. One paper titled 'Nurturing Ultra Special Senses in Future Leaders' was presented at the World Association of Social Psychiatry (WASP) 2015. The response at the conference encouraged me to introduce the concept to young adults who wish to train the brain for leadership and resilience. In matters of brain development, earlier is better. The immense potential of an adolescent brain is often lost because the lack of space within the cranium necessitates pruning away of unused circuits. Pattern thinking becomes entrenched in attitudes; hence, early intervention is desirable, yet it is never too late to tread the path of intentional brain training.

Abraham Maslow observed:

The unhappiness, unease and unrest in the world today are caused by people living far below their capacity.

Just reading this quote makes me feel very sad and my heart wrings itself out each time I hear of a brilliant young person who self-harms, degenerates into an addict or commits suicide. It reminds me that being immensely brilliant does not necessarily translate into an ability to cope.

Parents, coaches and mentors must keep an eye on the simultaneous development of emotional competences and intentionally ensure the building of resilience. While studying the Ultra Special Senses (named USSs for convenience hereafter), I was able to identify the processes that contribute to the building of the ability to bounce back from a setback, to persevere in rough times, and see the silver lining behind dark clouds and lead oneself back to wholehearted living.

WHY LEARN TO LEAD?

The need for a leader is organically embedded in pack animals. Leaders emerge spontaneously or through a ritualized process, but all members look up to the leader to stand firm, and be visible and communicative through a crisis. The resilience of a leader serves the whole community. Leadership is a quality worth developing in each individual because each one has to 'lead' a life and spontaneously take the 'lead' when a situation demands. Neurological competence circuits are laid and consolidated through practice. Leadership is not a single task or action, but a quality derived from the development of multiple circuits and competencies, each with its underlying neural circuitry. The work of neurological development and maintenance is never complete.

Neuroleadership consists of initiatives undertaken with knowledge of how the brain works, aimed at developing competencies essential for leadership in self or others.

Parents, teachers and coaches remember that children never listen to what parents 'say' but will faithfully copy whatever their parent 'do'. If the plan is to develop the next generation, we must begin with ourselves. We need to demonstrate restraint, resilience, balance and any of the qualities we wish to engender in others. I hope mentors, coaches and professionals will find actionable explanations in this book on topics we always knew existed and perhaps valued but were unaware that these can be intentionally enhanced. Now we know, we can.

ACKNOWLEDGEMENTS

The author gratefully acknowledges Professor Neeta Krishna for her help in editing *What's Your Superpower: Ultra Special Senses and You*. An old friend of the author from schooldays, Neeta was previously a professor of human resource development at Father Agnel Technical Education Complex, Vashi, Mumbai. Presently she is conducting programmes on creativity and entrepreneurship in Mumbai and other cities. She went through the first draft of this book with a fine-toothed comb and suggested many changes to make it reader-friendly.

Acknowledgement is due to the WASP for recognizing and showcasing the academic paper 'Nurturing Ultra Special Senses in Future Leaders' by Anjana Sen in its jubilee conference in London in 2014. The present work is based on this academic paper. The encouragement received at the conference was further boosted by Mr Gautam Sen, the author's life partner, who insisted that the content of the paper be made accessible and comprehensible to young readers who stand to gain the most from the work.

The author is grateful to late Mr Tejeshwar Singh of SAGE Publications and Mr Surit Mitra of Maya Publishers for recognizing her first work *Get the Ego Advantage!* published in 2006 by SAGE Publications. The SAGE India team has upheld the tradition of continuing a warm relationship with authors and contributors.

The author continues to learn from her coachees who have courageously turned their lives around demonstrating the power and impact of cognitive change in attitudes. Some of their journeys have been converted into anecdotes in this book, taking care to safeguard confidentiality.

INTRODUCTION

ULTRA SPECIAL SENSES

The famous five special senses have been stars in the realm of perception. Smell, taste, touch, sight and hearing are the sensations that keep us in touch with our surroundings and help us to understand the world. Animals, a term which includes humans, have developed highly specialized sense organs to convert energies of the environment into neural signals. These inputs are fed to the brain which processes and interprets them, recreating the experience as a sort of virtual reality within itself. This experience is a representation of the real environment and it serves as an essential survival system as it enables animals to acquire essential and preferred food or mates, to escape adverse conditions and evade predators.

Considering that each brain recreates its own reality, it becomes evident that each individual does savour a unique perspective based on unique perceptions and pre-occupations. Figure I.1 exemplifies how each brain filters information by passing it through subconscious factors to deliver a unique perception and perspective.

A differing perspective could result from a wayward special sense; for example, colour blindness or variation in connections can result in synaesthesia or hypersensitivity to input like sound. Altered perspective could arise due to a state of mind such as

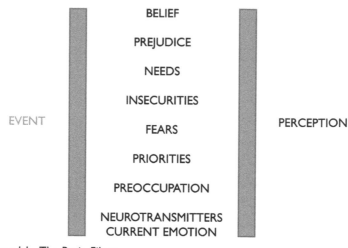

Figure I.I. The Brain Filter
Source: Author

hypervigilance, distrust, fatigue or the influence of intoxicants. Our five stars, the special senses, are certainly not alone in delivering experience, and we need to look past the dazzle of specialized organs of perception and examine some serious but quiet players which play perhaps an equal if not greater role in delivering a person's experience of life: senses which, while distinct from the big five, can have a reciprocal influence on them; senses we often discount and neglect; and senses that have evolved in response to humans patterns of life as social animals. These senses which I call Ultra Special Senses due to their externally indiscernible presence yet vital significance in the work of living are the subject of discussion of this book.

We are watchful about diminution of vision in the young and old alike, and take immediate steps to retrieve acuity, but we are not perturbed when the competence of empathy is lowered and we are rendered blind to the pain of our companions. What could be worse than losing sight, we exclaim, and someone who knows what sensory deprivation is (Helen Keller) replies 'Losing your Vision'.

EVOLUTION OF INDIVIDUALS IN REAL TIME

There is an evolutionary story told by brain architecture and function. Through successive stages of progression, the growth and refinement of the social way of life emerged that demanded new competencies. Social complexity gave rise to hierarchy, leadership, competition, collaboration and specialized roles. Living in society requires relationships and equations, discipline and restraint, empathy and enough intelligence to realize that individual identity thrives within the greater well-being of society. Aggression and superior muscle strength may be useful for single existence, but collaborative societies thrive instead of merely surviving.

To cope with the additional demand of functions of social living, the brain of social creatures grew, adding many layers on the top of the basic structure. Some existing circuits took on additional roles, so the design remained efficient and of reasonable proportion. Remarkably, a need for effective communication between members gave rise to new regions on the brain map, thereby increasing the total capacity. Copious networking allowed new and old regions to interact that led to great synergy.

A living growing brain is not just a historical fact. Every individual brain responds in real time to its experiences by adding cells, branches and synapses, consolidating well-used circuitry and pruning away unused parts. Charles Darwin warned us that it is not the fittest who survives but the most adaptable. Humans learn quickly when young, and habits and attitudes form and are established early. By the time humans enter the arena of competitive adulthood, some of their attitudes and patterns are found to be out of sync with the current times. Unlearning is thus as crucial to living as is learning. The exciting phenomenon of neuroplasticity—the discovery of continuously changing and rejuvenating neuronal circuits, making new connections and weakening old pathways—ensures that every brain evolves in real time, with each experience, repetition of an action and skill formation. At the end of each day, the circuits have changed by way of the number and efficiency of connections (synapses).

> *I can't go back to yesterday, because I was a different person then.*
> —Lewis Carroll in *Alice's Adventures in Wonderland*

A recent detection of neurogenesis, birth of neurons, in adults during research done in the 1990s opened up vistas of opportunity for intentioned growth. Some brains inherit strong circuits, but others can strengthen circuits and create new pathways where none existed or were lost due to trauma or disease:

- Some are born talented.
- Some develop talents and skills intentionally.
- Some are forced to develop skills due to circumstances.

Neuroplasticity always existed, but we only recognized it recently. Once proven, it seems to make perfect sense in hindsight and allows us to look forward at how we can use this knowledge. The human brain is in possession of many sensibilities other than those which merely deliver sensations. It may have been our ignorance that caused us to overlook their importance. Today, we have imaging techniques that allow us to study a working brain. Some research tools made available through state-of-the-art biophysical applications are safely non-invasive, enabling neuroscientists to design elegant studies and demonstrate results that are directly applicable to personal development. Collaborative interdisciplinary work is bringing closer, apparently diverse, medical disciplines such as neurology, psychiatry, psychology, endocrinology and immunology, and has generated new concepts such as neuroeconomics (where neuroscience meets psychology to explain how individuals make economic decisions) and neuroleadership (where knowledge about the neural substrate of competencies required in leadership can be applied to design exercises to develop these).

USSs that will be discussed in the following chapters are those faculties that have been researched to some extent under neuroscience. There are also references to studies conducted under the disciplines of behavioural studies, emotional intelligence and human resource development.

Ultra Special Senses: Intrinsic ability to perceive factors in the environment without the use of overtly apparent sense organs and to use the information constructively for personal as well as social well-being.

The aim of this book is to:

- Acknowledge USSs and their role.
- Understand where these senses reside and know ourselves better.
- Examine the contribution of these abilities towards building the attribute of resilience.
- Examine the requirement of such perceptiveness in actualizing full potential.
- Apply this knowledge in the development of the competence of leadership.
- Devise intentional methods of developing these senses to higher levels of acuity.

Thinking about how the brain works and finding ways to make it work best is an exercise in meta-awareness. For this, our brain has to contemplate itself, but luckily that is not too hard, and this book is written for readers who are unfamiliar with brain jargon. Understanding of how the brain works is useful because we use this organ all the time. Life, livelihood and relationships depend on it. Need we say more?

The best news to come out of the neuroscience laboratory is the proof of adult neurogenesis. We can now expect the birth of

Figure I.2. Ultra Special Senses
Source: Author

neurons in our brain every day and take action aimed at inviting the babies to join existing networks to strengthen and rejuvenate the whole. To attract newbies to join old circuits, we only need to stretch outside a comfort zone. I invite my readers to begin by expanding awareness about competence we take for granted and often don't bother to develop, like ability to put feelings aside and rise above sensory information such as annoyance for the sake of greater good through collaboration and teamwork. Fifteen such vital competencies will be discussed here.

The level of the brain where these perceptions are processed is roughly represented in Figure I.2. The lower levels below the horizontal line evolved early and are not easily accessed by reason and language. The higher level perceptions arranged above the horizontal line, representing the horizon between subconscious and conscious activity of the brain, are newer and involve intelligent circuits.

The brain has an architecture, and because it is a living organ it has to be nourished and cleared of metabolites. It has been

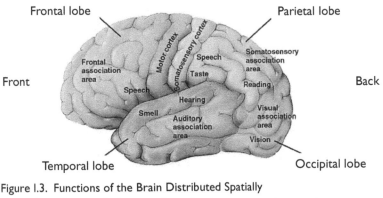

Figure I.3. Functions of the Brain Distributed Spatially
Source: https://www.mybraintest.org/brain-function-areas-structure-map/

described as a spatial organ, meaning that parts of it are dedicated to specific functions. Being a living thing, it changes with experiences, age, disease and recovery, often surprising the people who study it. Figure I.3 represents roughly what is meant when we call it a spatial organ. In this book, we discover locations for processes that we want to exercise and strengthen.

THE BRAIN IS FULL OF SURPRISES

At research laboratories, another recent and serendipitous discovery that has enhanced knowledge about the processes underlying social intelligence is the demonstration of the existence of 'mirror neurons'. This new knowledge has been used to treat chronic phantom pain in amputees. The mirror neuron has demystified phenomena such as empathy, emotional contagion, trust and thought reading, and it has enabled coaches to devise workouts to enhance these vital social competencies.

Seemingly strange collaboration between meditating monks and brain lab researchers has resulted in wondrous enlightenment. Their research has shown that many hours of meditation and exercise of compassion result in an increase in bulk of some specific lobes in the brain as well as changes in electrophysiology towards patterns of calmness and focus. Scientific studies add credibility to a coaches' repertoire of exercises that enhance specific functions of brain regions in an intentional and targeted fashion.

On a quest for enlightenment, a young seeker who happened to hear me saying 'it is never too early (nor too late) to begin developing USSs' has settled into my study. His name is Tan Tan and I haven't been able to send him away. I'm afraid, we will have to take him along with us through this book.

Here Tan Tan and I take the reader through subconscious and conscious levels of the brain to remind ourselves about hidden powers in the form of USSs following which we discuss how these abilities contribute to building resilience and to strengthen the fabric of leadership attributes.

TAN TAN HAS A
QUESTION ON VALUES

CHAPTER 1

VALUES ARE WHAT WE CARE DEEPLY ABOUT

Tan Tan* is somewhat annoying but wants to learn. He has heard that a lot of things worth learning may not be taught and is curious about what they may be.

Our friend Tan Tan wants to be a Ninja. Actually, he has no idea of what a Ninja is, and he has probably been watching too much TV. On probing, I realize that he wants to develop laser sharp intelligence and to be effective and efficient in crisis situations. I find this aspiration rather impressive and well in line with the concept of leadership, so I can't refuse when he enrols to be coached. I still find him annoying, though. His questions force me to keep my language jargon-free or at least jargon-depleted. In case you still find technical terms used that sound incomprehensible, you will find a glossary at the end of the book.

Tan Tan lives and studies in a monastery when he's not with me. His mentor, a monk and a teacher, has already impressed upon him the importance of building a strong body to connect with his bristling brain. That is why Tan Tan eats well and exercises every

---

* The name Tan Tan is a tribute to all the patients who contributed to brain science by being subjects of the study. The word 'Tan' is borrowed from Paul Broca's famous patient Louis Victor Leborne (1861) who had a lesion in the speech area of the brain that rendered him incapable of speaking except the one syllable 'Tan', although most of his other brain functions were intact.

day. Some of the exercises in his routine are for sharpening focus and concentration, to be more like some Ninja legends he has heard about. Each time he slackens on the exercises, he finds that he loses ground, but if he continues practice, quite suddenly the action becomes effortless. It's true for the muscle exercises and also for the ones that sharpen concentration!

Tan Tan is pleased each time he figures something out by himself. This feeling is a reward that is so personal that nothing on the outside of his skin can take it away. He finds it easy to think of the brain as a muscle, because muscles can feel the strain of effort and we can watch them grow. When I explained to him that brain cells follow the 'use it or lose it' principle, he said 'Aha' and decided that his 'brain is a muscle' analogy holds good because when we use a muscle, it strengthens, becomes efficient and gains bulk.

I shook my head, and said, 'Tan Tan, the brain is not a muscle. It's made of neurons not myocytes, and the brain is the boss because muscles won't move without directions from the brain to contract or relax'. But that only strengthened Tan Tan's notion that 'everything is connected' and now he was jumping up and down gleefully saying, 'Look my muscles get more energy when I am winning the argument!'. I, therefore, let his analogy (brain is a muscle) stay.

Another problem I have with Tan Tan looking over my shoulder as I type is that he brings words he learned from his teacher, who happens to be a monk, and demands that I explain those words with science. I may have protested, but I am the one who advocates un-specialization as a stage that is higher than specialization. Hence, I have brought upon myself the discomfort of stretching outside of a familiar territory to join some interdisciplinary dots.

Today, he demands to know what the word 'values' has to do with the brain because he heard his teacher saying, 'We need to be driven by values and not by emotions'.

Me: 'Values' are what we care deeply about.
Tan Tan: Like a friend?

Figure 1.1. Emotions Are Physiological States Mediated by Neurochemicals
Source: Author

Me: Not a person, an abstract concept like 'truth' or 'righteousness' and in the context of a friend 'loyalty'.

Tan Tan: Something fluffy that I cannot touch is supposed to 'drive' me?

Me: Emotions are temporary states; if you allow them to drive you, you will be all over the place. See the emojis in Figure 1.1, feelings change in an instant.

Tan Tan: And this 'righteousness' thing is more who I am? It is not even inside me!

Me: Abstract concepts are embedded in your person as what you care very much about.

THE FORGING OF HUMANS' VALUE SYSTEM

Life is a miraculous attribute of perishable yet successful organisms. There is a constant struggle to maintain life with its imperative needs on a planet with finite resources. Every organism must dynamically balance body chemistry and maintain itself within a magical range compatible with a healthy life. The result of this balance is called homeostasis (Changeux, Damasio, and Singer 2005). It is found as a critical feature in the tiniest single-cell amoeba as in complex multi-organ systems like ours. Needs are dictated by demands for resources from the environment for maintaining homeostasis. Among the requirements, some substances are in abundance and some are rare. The urgency of demand and availability or rarity pin the value of resources.

Humans live in groups for security, collaboration and development for common well-being. For animals that live in groups, social interaction and order are necessary and vital resources. Individuals and communities co-evolved codes of conduct and sharing to achieve stability (social homeostasis). Let us call it culture. The vital role of a community in survival and in co-creating quality of life does not allow culture to stray too far from biological value or the laws of nature. There is a collective quest for well-being and continuation of existing successful behaviours. Some values such as truth, humility, relationship and justice that have been tested through the ages and consistently found to win hearts are deeply ingrained in the psyche, thereby giving rise to a 'universal urge' to act in alignment with them.

Social values are an abstract concept of what is important and worth an effort to obtain. These fundamentally guide individual behaviour and therefore form the blueprint of conduct which includes the process of decision-making, inner dialogue and external manifestation, clearly visible to anyone who cares to look. Although many values are universal to all humans and faiths, individual variations in priorities and degree of motivation to pursue them result in unique combinations that represent the 'value print' of an individual. Humans may go through life without ever verbalizing their value system, but it manifests in behaviour, choices, passion and energy. Work done reflects the qualities (value print) of the doer just as ubiquitously as fingerprints. The artist can be identified from the work even if it carries no signature.

Tan Tan: I already have values before I know what that means?
Me: Embedded, but these can change with learning, role modelling
   and social conditioning.
Tan Tan: Then my conduct changes!

Variations occur due to exposure to influences such as values of caregivers in infancy, role models, peers, accepted teachers and life's experiences. Changes in core values bring about changes in personality and behaviour. Alignment with values generates enthusiasm and energy, whereas conflict with the core guidance system results in hesitation and emotional discomfort, even stress.

The experience of pain/pleasure as a consequence of social interaction acts as disincentive/incentive to correct the causal situation and regain social homeostasis. Distress, pain and pleasure (emotions) are biological and they indicate what is important, useful, desirable and/or valued. Emotions are mediated through neurotransmitters; these exert their influence on not just the brain but also on every cell and tissue. Thus, biological value encrypts itself upon social behaviour. The relationship works the other way around as well. Social requirements such as connection, belonging and purpose intertwine with the workings of the immune cells, circulatory system, attention and focus. So tight is the interplay that biology and social life are locked in dynamic embrace, making it hard to distinguish the plane of separation. If an individual is deprived of social connection, she/he suffers lowered immune status and various consequences, including withering of parts of the brain. Evidence of consequences of isolation is documented in studies on prisoners (Grassian 2006) and elderly reclusive persons (Singer 2018).

Tan Tan: I come to your study so you don't get sick from isolation.
Me: [*Sigh*] Thank you Tan Tan, but you said you come here to
   learn.
Tan Tan: That too, like I just learned that deep inside my brain,
   there is a box where I keep values, and how I arrange these makes
   me different from everyone, even from my 'guru'. These drive
   my arms and legs to do the work of values.

Me: Okay? How did the values get in that box?

Tan Tan: My mom, dad, granny and guru put them there, but I can shuffle them around myself.

Me: So, which one is right at the top of your box?

Tan Tan: Um, I don't know their names. But you know, I want very much to be a Ninja. You tell me!

Me: That only gives me a hint. It could be that you value effectiveness or maybe you value fairness. Do you get angrier when you see a leaking bucket being used to carry water or when I take a bigger share of chocolate?

Tan Tan: Oh! I get really mad when people say they're sharing but give me just a crumb!

Me: Then it's fairness you care about above effectiveness, though I'm still not sure if that's on top of your priority list, because only you would really know.

Tan Tan: [*Getting red in the face*] Why is this so hard to talk about?

Figure 1.2. Value Print
Source: Author

Me: Because the 'values' box is deep inside the brain and the spoken words are processed high up near the top of the head. Keep trying, you'll get better at this game. Everything is connected, remember! Make a short list from the examples in the diagram of 'Value Print' (Figure 1.2), and then give each one a priority number. That will introduce you to yourself, because that is your uniqueness.

Tan Tan: Look at these pictures of Tan Tan as a baby. I look very different now, but I still feel I am me each time. Why don't I feel like someone else, like the new person I become as I learn, and the funny person I look like as I grow? Were you ever a young girl?

Me: Yes, I was! And I was cute.

Tan Tan: Mmm... that's hard to imagine, but did you feel like you on the inside?

Me: Tan Tan, you're getting ahead of me. We learn that in the next chapter when we talk about the 'sense of self'. It's the first of the Ultra Special Senses!

USS 1

CONSCIOUSNESS AND SENSE OF SELF

CHAPTER 2

BEING GOOD AT
BEING ME

Me: Tan Tan, please be still and apply your mind to what I'm discussing.

Tan Tan: My mind? I'm upside down just now, but my mind is right side up!

Me: Tan Tan, I get distracted with your handstands, please settle down.

Tan Tan: You have to learn to focus. My mind is ready.

Me: Ownership of a mind is a sensation. This sensation projects itself to body parts and perceives the skin as an envelope that contains personhood.

Tan Tan: I am a sensation?

Me: In Antonio Damasio's words, 'The mind is a flow of mental images'. The brain functions like a symphony whose performance generates its own conductor. The sensors of touch, temperature and pressure from the skin, a wealth of signals converted from light and sound from the environment are used to assemble a virtual universe with a protagonist (self) in its midst as a point of reference. The spaces and forms the mind assembles are represented in brain maps.

The brain is a spatial organ, like an office. It has places in which distributed work is organized. When we want to move a limb, there is a dedicated clutch of neurons that do just that. There is a location where memories are stored—sensory areas with a proportionate representation for the highly sensitive skin of the hands and a much smaller area that represents touch from the skin of the back—and the whole visual-field map is arranged around the back of the brain. A spectacular consequence of the brain's incessant and dynamic mapping gives rise to the mind. There are maps of everything:

- Inside the body
- Outside the body
- Concrete/abstract
- Present/previously recorded
- Feelings (body states)
- Spatial and temporal relationships
- Actions

Tan Tan: Wow! How many neurons do I have?

Me: A hundred billion or more.

Tan Tan: Where in the brain map do I live?

Me: At some point in evolution, organisms had enough brain tissues to generate consciousness which seems inexorably linked with a sense of personhood and tethered to the body map. Although the body grows and changes morphology, the 'person' does not change but generates an autobiography. Perhaps the sameness is maintained through homeostatic mechanisms (processes that help to revert body chemistry to default settings) because they deliver a more stable frame of reference than body morphology which changes as we grow and age; yet the body must form a part of the self for reasons of survival and health which when ensured, nourish the neurons and maintain consciousness.

Tan Tan: No body, no consciousness; no consciousness, no self.

Me: Self consists of the following (Damasio 2012):

- Proto-self: Stable body signals with primordial feelings
- Core-self: Related to interaction with objects and other creatures

• Autobiographical-self: Integrates the dynamic pulses that make up the core-self to organize past memories and project plans for the future

The core-self and autobiographical-self together become the 'knower' and seem to be the owner of a flow of imagery called the 'mind'.

Tan Tan: Excuse me Damasio, can you explain in Tan Tan?
Me: One, proto-self is Tan Tan the 'creature'. Two, core-self is Tan Tan the 'being' which is different from every other being and object. Three, autobiographical-self is Tan Tan who has been around for a while and has been learning and remembering. All together you are you.
Tan Tan: Yeah, I'm already good at being me.
Me: The famous five special senses with their highly specialized receptor organs bring a spectrum of information from the environment into the body and brain. Together they reconstruct a virtual world for the rudimentary self to live in. The self is a projection of a reasonably stable frame of reference tethered to the body, thereby creating an experience of discreet identity which has a hardwired need for interdependence with other members of the species due to inherent vulnerability. Sense of self is closely linked with consciousness which is knowledge of one's own existence and the existence of surroundings. Emotions are closely linked with consciousness too. These are experiences of bodily feelings from a first-person perspective. Neurological lesions that cause the loss of consciousness also obliterate emotions.

Each individual's world is a perception reconstructed from the data collected by the 'senses' (Ramachandran 2004). The perspective could be unique for each person. The conscious knower has a sense of agency, a perception of the body being commanded by its mind.

Both consciousness and sense of self take a break during deep dreamless sleep and anaesthesia. These are states of vulnerability, leading to the surmise that consciousness and sense of self evolved as a protective mechanism. The wakefulness mechanism known as the reticular formation is located close to the proto-self nuclei in the brainstem. Damage to the brainstem related to this area manifests as coma.

Tan Tan: The brain has a stem?

Me: Imagine the brain as a blooming flower at the end of a long stalk (the spinal cord). Right where the stalk swells to meet the flower; let's call that the brainstem. The structures passing through are vital.

Brain work (electrical activity) within the topmost and most recently evolved part of the brain (neocortex) is mostly conscious. If it occurs in words, interpretation of feelings or imagined visuals, we call them 'thoughts'. These occur randomly in response to observed events or recollection. It is important to remember that living things connect with the environment through the senses. The brain may overfunction and create experiences that do not have an external stimulus. This can happen if triggered by chemicals generated by emotions or by neuroactive substances and drugs or by disease processes.

Tan Tan: Ok, so the knower is me who owns the mind. The awake brain works all together to create a mind through many many maps, and they may not be correct because we got high on weed or got an infection!

Me: Or because I overthink, strain the brain and lose perspective!

Tan Tan: So everyone has a mind, but everyone doesn't use it right. They should teach this in school.

Me: Living things deliberately seek out conditions of well-being, a broadening of the basic goal of survival. Just surviving is not enough; we must thrive. Most homeostatic balancing, like keeping blood sugar and hormones at optimal levels, is done non-consciously.

Tan Tan: Whoa! Wait a minute! I got this much; sense of self is conscious. What is this non-conscious? You mean subconscious, don't you? I've heard that when the guru talks with older monks. Tell me tell me!

Me: Consider the computer; I touch a key, and a letter appears on the screen. It is the letter I wanted and will use it to create a sentence that expresses my thought to the reader. I am not aware about the work that goes into the process of converting a touch on the keyboard into a shape and how it graphically appears on the screen. If I had to figure out how to do this, I would not have the luxury of thinking up the next word I need to use. A similar process in my brain is guiding the semantics of my sentence. The grammar I learned as a child has been encrypted and is working now. The work that happens below the level of awareness is enormous. For each muscle that I wilfully contract, a set of others have to relax and stabilize the joint to allow the movement to be smooth and elegant.

Executing the same movements many times over helps the oft-used circuits to become more efficient. Speed of transmission within practised circuits is enhanced and its connections consolidated functionally. Once the practised activity neurons begin to fire efficiently and fast, the activity becomes converted into a 'skill' and demands less conscious attention and energy for its execution. This lowered requirement for attention frees up space in the neocortex, and the free neurons can then be used to conduct other tasks, and the skilled task is conducted without attentiveness.

Remember the attention required to coordinate hands, feet and back muscles during your first bike riding lesson and the ease and balance with which you ride after many hours of practice. More functions of the brain occur without awareness than the conscious ones.

The architecture of the brain has followed evolution and placed the thinking parts closer to the top of the skull cavity (cranium). It is a top-heavy design. Thinking requires a lot of connecting, and connections slow down the signals. We can use the iceberg analogy, where only the visible tip is conscious. The rest of the brain works below the radar of awareness. Let us glance at some activities within the subconscious; think of these as apps that continue to run in the background:

- Emotions
- Experience of threat and reward (ego, pain, hurt)
- Assumptions, stereotypes, prejudice
- Belief, confidence
- Values and fears
- Wisdom
- Hope
- Vital functions and homeostatic control mechanisms

Tan Tan: Why have the subconscious when we're unaware of it?
Me: To have a significant conscious tip the iceberg needs a massive submerged presence.

The subconscious processes are the ones that make life worth living. Therein lie motivation, aspiration and values that guide externally expressed behaviour.

The subconscious brain is swift, efficient and untiring—the real rockstar. The conscious brain is lazy and suffers from a presumptive bias. It looks for the proof of what the subconscious believes.

However, the conscious system is capable of diligent analysis and can reset the beliefs stored in the subconscious and reorganize values and fears. It can re-examine prejudice and turn it around. But in order to do all this, it has to become aware of what lies in the subconscious.

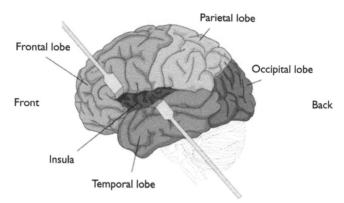

The insula is visible only after retracting the frontal and temporal lobes

Figure 2.1. Lobes of the Human Brain
Source: https://www.kenhub.com/en/library/anatomy/insula-en

Tan Tan: Now you want me to become aware of what I'm unaware! Why was I made unaware in the first place?

Me: For the purpose of efficiency and alacrity.

Tan Tan: How do I dip into the subconscious?

Me: The bridge between the conscious and subconscious systems exists as a lobe within the temporal region called the insula (See Figure 2.1).

The insula is used and developed when we practise eye–hand coordination, mindfulness and sports that demand focused attention. It is also exercised when we practice empathy and feel compassion for others. Once strong enough, we can use the insula to introspect and become aware of what we are habitually unaware. This practice opens up the path to access our own wisdom, which otherwise may lie unused, ensconced deep in the realm of wordless mystery.

Being a spatial organ, activity in the various regions of the intelligent tissue may plod along without excitement, but the penny drop and 'eureka' moment happens in the subconscious. If the conscious brain is buzzing and noisy, it may not hear the penny drop.

To hear our own wisdom, the conscious brain needs to be quietened.

Quietening the thinking brain is attempted through meditative and calming practices like mindfulness, and guided processes like chanting, rituals, visualization and music. Meditators, mindful sportspersons, dancers and musicians have well-developed insula lobes.

The sense of self is so very fundamental and deeply installed in the brain that we as coaches need not worry about developing or strengthening this sense. Sense of self drives the basic instincts of self-preservation and self-defence.

Tan Tan: I told you, I'm already good at being me.

This sense places each person in the centre of her/his own universe and makes the individual perceive disproportionate importance and thus delusional in relation to the world around the person. The brainstem is anatomically far away from the layers that think, evaluate and analyse.

Tan Tan: But everything is connected!
Me: You're very correct Tan Tan. The intelligent processes can reach down here and explain where we really stand with respect to the world.

Tan Tan: [*Becoming sad*] I don't feel important. Elders treat me like a stupid child!

Me: You are a child, but not stupid at all! Your brain is growing at a dizzy speed!

Tan Tan: Will they treat me better if I am tall and handsome, or if I'm smart at studies? Or (making snake eyes) when I am dangerous like a Ninja?

Me: [*Uncomfortably*] Older people will treat you better when they learn how they interact with a child today is what will count in the future. A child learns about what she/he is worth based on the respect or contempt conveyed by significant elders.

Tan Tan: The message may be untrue!

SELF-WORTH

The phenomenon of self-worth, a perception about the importance of self in relation to other occupants of life outside of self, is what we must engage with and absorb the importance of. Persons in positions of authority make indelible impact on the self-worth of persons in submissive roles. The quantum of self-worth an individual perceives is pivotal to her/his development as an individual and as a member of society. Even if we have ensured the installation of good values through example and education, a person with low self-worth can stoop to compromise those values for short-term gains like peer approval. When one has compromised an embedded value, she/he falls even lower in the assessment of self, setting off a spiralling disappointment and self-loathing. Self-worth of individuals sets the standards for integrity in society as it all adds up. An individual who holds herself/himself in high esteem feels secure enough to refuse a tempting opportunity to indulge, having savoured the sensation of high self-worth, she/he prefers not to trade it for popularity, ego satisfaction or easy pleasure. Self-worth is the belt which straps values safely in the driver's seat. Wear this seat-belt always, even for short journeys. Occasionally check on how strong it is.

Self-worth is the cornerstone of self-love. It is impossible to love yourself if you don't believe you're worth it. A low self-worth person does not accept love from self or from others.

> *We accept the love we think we deserve.*
> —Stephen Chbosky

This affects the quality of relationships and the reciprocation of love that sometimes never occurs. A person who does not know how to love herself/himself has no clue about how to love another.

When we are young, our caregivers ensure that each time we suffer a lowering of self-worth through a mistake or a failure, we refill the tank of precious self-assessment and regain the feeling of being worthy. When we grow up, we need to learn to do this on our own, because of the following reasons:

- It keeps our values safe.
- It helps us uphold integrity.
- It helps us accept and give love.
- It ensures we reach full potential by aiming high.
- It generates confidence to grab opportunities in time.

If we are treated in a way that makes us feel worthless as children, we tend to believe that.

Tan Tan: Mom makes me feel important!

Me: It may be useful to develop tools to assess how we feel about our worthiness in real time, because it can wax and wane with situations and experiences. Try using the Self-Worth Meter (Figure 2.2) to express how you feel about your worth just now. Once we make ourselves aware about our current level, we can take the matter seriously enough to find time and energy and pay attention to the process of resurrecting self-regard. The usual way that we 'feel' is through emotions. Low self-worth broadly feels

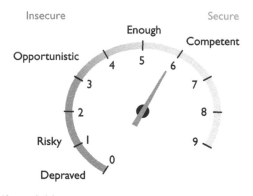

Figure 2.2. Self-worth Metre
Source: Author

'bad', and the bad may not bubble up to the conscious level. Being unaware of a feel-bad does not block the consequences of the long-term presence of hyperactive chemicals of the 'bad' spectrum. They lower immune status and hamper healing or growth in all tissues. To be safe and healthy, try to stay in the secure right half of this semi-circular measuring scale

Tan Tan: Why is there no number 10 on your metre?

Me: There's no such thing as too much self-respect.

Tan Tan: I know people who think the world about themselves.

Me: How would we know what someone else thinks? This metre is for personal use, but be truthful to yourself!

Tan Tan: There's no need to say that; everyone is honest with themselves.

Me: Not true. You experienced how hard it is to name your values. We often profess and practise different values.

Tan Tan: Okay, so I have a measuring metre and I scored 3 out of 9 (grows quiet and pensive).

Baww, I want my Mommy!

Self-esteem isn't everything; it's just that
there's nothing without it.

—Gloria Steinem

Me: The methods used to crank up lowered self-worth can vary and be customized for each individual. Here, try some of these:

- Remind yourself about your achievements.
- Refocus on goals.
- Reconnect with the love and respect received from friends.
- Reconnect with faith.
- Renew belief in your own competence.
- Practise and better existing skills.
- Seek guidance and training.
- See failure as an opportunity.

Time and energy spent on self-worth-healing is of fundamental importance to both the individual and society as the strength of this safety belt of self-worth is what translates as the integrity of a society.

A 30-year-old executive Raj has a wonderful career opportunity. He has to leave home to join the assignment in a week. His family consists of two sisters. One sister Ananya has a problem with social adjustment. The week before leaving home is unpleasant between Raj and Ananya. She entices him to come to blows, but he restrains himself. She provokes him further by resorting to violent behaviour, in response to which he hits out blindly. His blows result in the sister sustaining a scalp wound that bleeds copiously. The drama continues with a police report and restraining order. Raj leaves home and city knowing that he cannot return, consumed with guilt and remorse. He cannot forgive himself for being violent. He now hates himself. He joins the new assignment, finds an apartment and begins work. Raj hates every moment of the work, he finds the apartment oppressive and cannot make new friends. He pines for his hometown hangouts, old friends and familiar food. The overall low mood results in poor quality of work. Physically he feels underconfident because he experiences a thumping in the chest and panic-like circulation. He begins to believe that he has heart disease and refuses challenging tasks. He spends all free time consulting doctors and undergoing investigations.

He has already decided to resign from this job as his contribution is not appreciated. He just wants to somehow go back to the town he grew up in. The flare-up with Ananya and subsequent restraining order mean that even if he does return, he cannot live in the family home. Raj says, 'He has no will to live'. Raj and I worked on his attitude towards himself. Initially, on the self-worth metre, he assessed his score as 1. Gradually, he built it up to 5. His work output improved and the appreciation he received helped to sustain the improvement. On the third session, Raj said 'I no longer feel the urge to end my life'.

Tan Tan: Whoa! I didn't think that he was suicidal.

Me: He said that he had no will to live.

Tan Tan: I didn't take that seriously.

Me: Low self-worth results in self-harm. Resigning from a job on impulse, abusing alcohol and other drugs, indulging in unsafe sex, promiscuity, recklessness and taking on unnecessary risks, all of this qualifies as self-harm. When a parent sends a child away to seek a life, if equipped with a secure level of self-worth, the child can be considered to be safe.

Tan Tan: Aah, that's why you say self-worth is a safety belt!

Me: The next step in growing up is to learn to transcend self. That's a tough cookie, especially if we have unknown unmet needs.

Tan Tan: I need a cookie.

USS 2
SENSE OF BELONGING

CHAPTER 3

CAN I BELONG TO A PLANET?

At the playground this morning Tan Tan runs to me in tears. His sobs are coming from a very deep place and shaking his whole frame.

Tan Tan: [*Between sobs*] Nobody wants me in their team; how will I play?

He turns and runs after another boy in a team uniform and tugs at his clothes.

Tan Tan: [*Begging*] Please let me in play with your team, any team! [*It's pathetic!*]

Me: Tan Tan, here, come here. You can be a member of the 'watchers'; see, all of us are here in the stands and we're watching! There, you see my friend wearing spectacles? He's the captain of 'watchers' and says, 'Tan Tan is a great watcher, get him here!'

Tan Tan settles down reluctantly and snuggles close. He looks suddenly tiny and crumpled. In a few minutes he is enjoying the game and seems to be filling out, as if recovering from an illness.

The sense of self enlarges joyously with group acceptance and wilts in the insecurity that comes with isolation. Belonging augments survival in evolutionary history, which is why banishment is interpreted as a death sentence, ostracism causes massive anxiety and being excluded from a group activity is hurtful. The hugely successful evolutionary strategy of belonging laid the primordial architecture of neuronal circuitry; hence, this need is hardwired too deeply for the intelligence to circumvent or transcend. Tan Tan relaxed only after finding an alternative group to identify with.

Isolation is found to hamper the production of myelin in the brain—an effect that is found to be reversed after socialization. Myelin is the fatty material that sheathes nerves and improves the conduction and effectiveness of signalling. Children who suffer social isolation display cognitive and social impairments as adults. Recent studies (Makinodan et al. 2012) suggest that there is a critical period during brain maturation when isolation may lead to white matter deficiency in the pre-frontal cortex (PFC) of humans, a region that participates in working memory and manifests in actualization of general intelligence.

The feeling of belonging is mediated by the hormone and neurotransmitter oxytocin. It has many functions in interpersonal interaction, sex, birthing and letting down of milk in mammals. Oxytocin is the neurochemical of intimacy. Secretion of oxytocin occurs at many neuronal levels, including the hypothalamus, but the main factory is the posterior pituitary gland (endocrine master gland). Oxytocin is also called 'bonding hormone'; it generates feelings of trust, generosity and loyalty. It can reduce stress and improve heart function apart from its beneficial effects of improved conductivity of the brain.

Belonging is thus a biological need as much a driver of behaviour as hunger and sex.

Tan Tan: Do you think they'll sign me on if I cut my hair like they do?

Me: Come on Tan Tan, next you'll bend over backwards and work like a slave for them.

Tan Tan: [*Turning contemplative*] Did I make a fool of myself?

Me: A pathetic sort of fool!

Tan Tan: What was I thinking! I felt so weak, like I could get energy if I wear that team shirt!

Me: In every situation, we instinctively look for something, and it may not be the same thing we look for in another, or even when the same situation crops up again. Here Tan Tan, you were looking to be one with the team and play.

If we get what we are looking for, we feel fulfilled or satisfied, but if that prize eludes us, we are left with a feeling of despondency and the whole process can happen without us being aware. When we raise our level of emotional awareness, we can be more in touch with what motivates us in the particular moment, and we can understand the feeling of dejection or elation that follows. Have you felt like that before?

Tan Tan: I feel weak like that when the elders send me off without listening to my questions.

Me: There are a lot of things we can want from an interaction, and when we don't get that, we feel low. Being in touch with the subconscious helps us to communicate with the owner of the mind and find out what I feel is the important need right now.

Self-awareness is empowered by enabling purposeful action and efficient use of energy, as well as helping us to recover faster from a put-down. We also spend less time and energy in ruminating and wondering 'What was I thinking!'

When we're disconnected from the subconscious, it goes about its business anyway because the self lives in the subconscious, and the separation between the conscious and subconscious makes the intelligence feel that it is not in charge and it becomes despondent.

To begin with, we can recall and examine a past incident to find answers to the question: What was I thinking!? As we get better, awareness kicks in and can be applied in real time. Awareness connects subconscious self and conscious intelligence so that both can function collaboratively.

The question to ask yourself instead of the plaintive 'What was I thinking' is 'In that particular instance or interaction what was it that I was looking for?' Was it:

1. Significance/wanting to feel valued
2. One up/feel better about myself/judgemental
3. To assist
4. Make my own decisions/control/be right
5. Stay safe/avoid change
6. To intimidate/defend/hurt back
7. Belonging/inclusion/acceptance/validation
8. Opportunity/prospects/thrills
9. Empathy/to communicate what I feel
10. To make the world a better place
11. To understand/solve a problem/find out the truth

When we perform this exercise about 10 times with 10 situations and find a recurring theme, that will bring to the fore one or more of our persistent needs.

Deeply fundamental human needs, if unmet, have a profound effect on physical and mental well-being. Unmet needs are like gaping holes in our being that exert a vacuum like pull on the environment. Vacuums are not discerning about quality. Needy persons grab whatever they find in the vicinity and draw it into their lives. Take the example of the need for attention. This is a form of the basic need for connection. When parents are not paying attention to a child; she/he tries whatever she/he can to enter their focus. When nothing works, she/he destroys something or harms herself/himself and creates an emergency situation. This succeeds in getting her/him what she/he was looking for, to be seen, heard and acknowledged. She/he resorts to this behavioural pattern repeatedly. To her/his vacuum, getting yelled at or punished is more acceptable than being overlooked. The quality of attention she/he is receiving is unhealthy and has its own consequences like lowered self-esteem and poor expectations of self.

Anu, a 30-year-old professional, came to me with a history of frequent breakdowns with excessive crying, leading to unconscious spells. The breakdowns were way out of proportion to the triggers and had started affecting her work. While interviewing her, I found that she discovered that she was an adopted child late in her teens. Her mother was very sick at the time and she died soon after. Her father who was much older passed away within a year of the mother's death. Anu had a flourishing career, and looked up to her mentor at work with great respect. Her world came crashing down when the mentor turned a sexual predator. She resigned from the job. She lost the membership of the organization that seemed like home and felt revolted by the experience with the person she had considered a father figure. Anu set up her own business that she worked hard at and is now running successfully. She is well off financially, has a home and many suitors. Her breakdowns and crying spells are now taking a toll on her relationships. Her boyfriend began verbally abusing her, but she clung to him till he took the initiative to leave her. Within a week, she had a new boyfriend who was good to her, but was frightened by her bouts of crying. He was afraid that she might harm herself and was feeling trapped in the situation. In this relationship, Anu was the abuser, emotionally coercing the young man to stay, threatening to self-harm and criticizing him for not giving her the solace she needed. After cognitive intervention, Anu is learning to transfer her need for roots to a feeling of belonging to her industry and fraternity of professionals. Her meltdowns are now fewer and less dramatic, and she has picked up enough courage to honourably end her unhappy and inadequate relationship, and has big plans for the future.

Tan Tan: Anu is a grown-up person and doesn't know that she doesn't have what she needs! I don't want to make a fool of myself and be pathetic about getting into the team, but I do need to feel accepted. What to do?

Me: Consider yourself a member of a group you can't be thrown out of.

Tan Tan: Family is a group—right?

Me: Yes, but we can get divorced or disinherited. In patriarchal cultures, girls are told even when they're quite little that the family they thought was theirs is not where they belong. That is a cruel revelation for any child.

Tan Tan: That's terrible!

Me: Family elders often lay down conditions for acceptance. They dictate what clothes to wear, what profession to choose, what grades to get at school, who you must marry, how to spend your money, where to live....

Tan Tan: Oww! The cool gangs at school have rules too. A Ninja can't belong to cool school gangs. What to do? Where to belong?

Me: With reasonable restrictions like having to obey laws, you can be a citizen of a town and a country. But you can enlarge the container.

Tan Tan: Ummm! Can I belong to the planet?

Me: Yes yes, of course you can! You do belong to the planet! You're connected with the molecules outside your body through the air you breathe, water, food, and you give back molecules to the air and soil. It's a continuous relationship of give and take and a pretty harmonious one too! This connection is more vital than a connection with another human, which we hanker after and ignore our essential requirement for what we need from our planet. We didn't drop on to the earth's surface from outside, we emerged from the earth and will go back into it.

Tan Tan and I were giving high fives to each other and anyone else we met all day! We felt connected to everything and everyone, imagined ourselves expanded and buoyant like balloons!

Tan Tan: I feel so free! Just this morning I was willing to be a slave just to be accepted in a basketball team, and I don't even like basketball! I was even thinking of getting a weird hairdo because it felt like I would die....

Me: Oh that's a brain funk. Clever design of 'survival strategy'. Humans are herd animals. We're safe in communities. When we lived in tribes long ago, separation from the safety of the tribe did result in death in the wild. A human who could sense risk of death in isolation would stick to the tribe and live to pass on those genes. You have those very successful genes.

Tan Tan: There is a need for belonging, and the 'sense' of belonging fills that need. Then I don't feel the need to please everyone.

Me: This sense is also embedded too deep for intelligent processes to override. So let's just accept it. The problem with the deeper USSs is that we tend to overlook their power over us. Then we feel stupid and exclaim 'What was I thinking!'

Tan Tan: Because I can't override it, I have to find a bigger club to belong to. I'm so glad I chose to belong to the planet Earth, it will always be the same.

Me: Er… no; how can you be certain? Planet scale changes are devastating for us humans.

Tan Tan: [*Shocked*] Earthquake!

Tan Tan: [*Bawling*] I don't want to die … waaah!

Me: The deepest USS, the sense of self, developed so strongly that it drives the instinct for survival. We don't want to break that, do we? Along with it (homeostasis—going back to how things were) comes a wish for permanence which is why each time we are reminded of death, we experience dejection. Intelligence easily comprehends the reality of death, but the deep-seated wish for immortality continues to wield influence, pushing its agenda in the form of denial. Notice how we repeatedly forget that we are mortal. Finding the fountain of youth and earning a boon of immortality feature prominently in myths and legends, and modern-day research continues the hunt for ways to beat death. Coping mechanisms evolved equally deeply within brain circuits, to balance out the ingrained fear of death and discomfort with uncertainty. That coping strategy is known as the 'sense of hope', also known as *faith*. Before discussing *hope*, let's refer to Table 3.1 that describes basic human needs and how they translate into behaviour while we look for the fulfilment of unmet needs. The column on the right gives suggestions for getting over toxic attitudes and desperate reactiveness.

Table 3.1. Basic Human Needs

Basic Need	What I Was Looking for in That Incident	How I Can Try to Fulfil the Need in a Healthy Way
Connection	Belonging Acceptance Validation of behaviour Conformity Empathy Communicate what I feel Try to please	Enlarge my concept of community so that the risk of separation from a smaller clan feels less frightening.
Certainty	Security Resist change Avoid risk Keeping hope alive Retaining faith	Accept the reality that life is uncertain. Accept inevitable phenomenon of death and disease and other influences that are outside individual control. Build faith in own competence as that is well within our own circle of influence. Build scientific temper.
Esteem	Prove I am right One up/compete/shaming Feel better about myself Fix blame Judge Show off	Review habits of comparing, criticizing, blame fixing, perfectionism, proving. Build self-assurance through accurate self-assessment.
Autonomy	My way Agreement Control Subjugation	Review hierarchical structure in society and accept my present position. Become aware of the boundaries I need to respect. Develop democratic and affiliative styles of leadership. Work towards developing myself for the position I aspire to.

Basic Need	What I Was Looking for in That Incident	How I Can Try to Fulfil the Need in a Healthy Way
Self-actualization	Opportunity Collaboration/ interdependence Prospects Validation of held belief Be useful to others Understanding concepts Solving problems Being fair and just Creating purpose	Create purpose. Ask 'why' and check alignment with values. Learn to witness the self and keep self in perspective. Set clear goals. Take pride in the present role. Train for the next level. Practise mindfulness and compassion.

Source: Author

USS 3

SENSE OF HOPE
AKA FAITH

Hope May Be Irrational, But It Prevails

CHAPTER 4

DOCTOR BELIEF AT WORK WITH NURSE HOPE

T he word 'hope' is used both as a verb and as a noun. Here we discuss the phenomenon of hope as a biological process of desire that has an element of belief of fulfilment. Experimentally, 'expectation of reward' is considered as hope (Rowe et al. 2008). Reward in humans is a complex mechanism (salutary/monetary/sexual), but expectation is essentially a representation of the future events involving a likelihood of reward. The phenomenon is observable on functional magnetic resonance imaging (fMRI) as an activation of certain brain regions, mainly the medial frontal cortex. The lateral frontal, parietal and temporal cortices also participate in specific conditions. Another observable enhancement occurs in connectivity within the PFC positively influencing cognition in the brain. The presence of hope is thus beneficial to brain function regardless of whether hope is founded on actually realizable occurrence.

The act of receiving treatment for illness or for the relief of symptoms sets off a 'hope' or expectation of recovery. Relief of pain or even biochemical changes effecting true recovery are found to occur after receiving inactive tablets or pills. This is known as the 'placebo effect' and found to be very real and not occurring only in gullible people but across the population. The activation of nucleus accumbens the reward centre with concomitant release of dopamine was detected during the administration of placebo (Scott et al. 2007). Persons who exhibited this activation also experienced pain reduction.

Hope delivers dopamine which has a positive effect on cognition and arousal. It improves working memory enhancing intelligence. Although hope hinges on expectation in the future, its presence has a beneficial effect on brain function in the present. This makes evolutionary sense because what the individual plans, decides and executes in the present pans out to make the expectation come true in the future. Although the expected result may not come around, the benefit to the brain and body through a dollop of dopamine is assured. The presence of hope engenders positive emotions such as courage and feels empowering with improved brain performance and motivation.

Mrs D, 79 years old, a strong woman, widowed 30 years ago, has lived independently and steadfastly refused to move in with her daughters who are similarly strong and fiercely independent. They care for her diligently but from a distance, to respect her wishes. Mr D lived a healthy life until he suffered a fracture of the femur. Being thus immobilized, he developed complications and died quite suddenly due to pulmonary embolism. At 79, Mrs D had a fall inside her home and was rushed to the hospital. When she heard that the diagnosis was a fracture of the femur, just as it had been in the case of her husband, she believed that it was her turn to die. Medical Science has advanced enough to deal with her fracture effectively and prevent embolism. She was helped to walk on the second day after surgery. Her recovery was satisfactory and the surgeon sent her home with instructions to keep up physiotherapy. Back at home, Mrs D refused to walk. Physiotherapists visited each day and coaxed her out of bed. They found her muscle strength adequate and kept encouraging as did her loving family and friends. Yet her quality of life deteriorated as did her mood. When asked why she did not even move her arms while in bed, though she was able to sign cheques quite legibly, she replied, 'My time has come'. Her daughters tried very hard to change that belief, but they lost her to lung complications in one year's time.

In terminally ill persons, the presence of hope has inexplicable influence on recovery, pain perception and quality of life. When people lose hope, their lives deteriorate rapidly along with setback in health. Dr Viktor Frankl, an Austrian neurologist and psychiatrist as well as a Holocaust survivor, has recorded his observations of persons detained in concentration camps. One inmate had an inexplicable belief that the war will end on Christmas. Christmas passed by and the war continued. The person succumbed to a chronic infection within a fortnight, though he had harbored that infection for months before Christmas.

Tan Tan: Do you believe in life after death?

Me: No, I don't. But you are free to believe what you find empowering.

Tan Tan: I think I'll stick to science; it makes a lot of sense. My teacher says I'm smart, so I'm sure I will understand.

Me: Science has explained that sense of self is essential for maintaining the strongest instinct of survival. Fear of death is only a manifestation of the same instinct—the flip side of that coin. The fear of death is perceived just as strongly as the preference to remain alive. To accept mortality, we need to understand that the built-in aversion is essential, but it does not prolong life expectancy. When we come around to accept mortality, one life may seem quite enough.

BELIEF

Tan Tan has developed a belief in his own abilities through the messages conveyed to him by his mentor. When he said 'My teacher says I am smart, so I'm sure I will understand', I gathered he truly believes the teacher and will prove him right. Much of the communication of the mentor's faith in the unrealized potential of the mentee is conveyed not through words but through the hint of respect conveyed through body language.

This is the seed of self-belief. This will serve him well as he grows up. On the way, his abilities will be tested in the real world and with every tiny achievement, faith in his own abilities will be consolidated. There will be setbacks when he tries and fails, but the momentum set by the positive expectations of people we regard with respect helps us to learn from setbacks and press on and overcome obstacles. In this way, we refill the treasure chest of belief. Once familiar with what confidence feels like, we can wean ourselves away from the expectations of others and continue on our own. Wordless transfer of expectations about hitherto unrealized potential between persons usually flows from one in a position of accepted authority to those in submissive roles, like parent to child, teacher to student and boss to subordinate. The phenomenon has been named 'Pygmalion effect'.

Named after the Greek myth of Pygmalion and its interpretation by George Bernard Shaw in his play *Pygmalion*, and studied and reported by Robert Rosenthal and Lenore Jacobson as early as 1968, the positive effect of high expectation from people in authority upon individual performance is a well-documented phenomenon. Studied mostly in a teacher–student setting, it has been found to hold true in leader–follower scenarios. The subordinate rises to fulfil that expectation. The same is true for negative expectation, and in the negative form, it is named 'Golem effect' (from Jewish mythology) also named by Rosenthal, Babad and Inbar (Babad 1982). The phenomenon is also called 'self-fulfilling prophecy', and every teacher and leader should be aware of the power of this prophecy.

Inadvertent non-verbal cues are most probably responsible for raising/lowering self-esteem of a subject, thereby spurring her/him on to achieve in line with the expectation conveyed subconsciously. The phenomenon could be leveraged as a vital leadership tool, while awareness could prevent the Golem effect by taking care not to convey what is not intended.

Tan Tan: You're saying expectation is not expressed in words, but I carry some around very deep in my brain box—expectations of how I will turn out as I grow. But things don't happen according to plan! Things just happen like my friend Hari's accident. Now both his legs don't work. That's not fair! The man who knocked him down was drunk.

Me: Life is uncertain.

Tan Tan: I hate that!

Me: All humans hate that. We cope with that discomfort of uncertainty by creating a belief.

Tan Tan: Like God?

Me: Yes. We start with the same beliefs our family has been carrying.

Tan Tan: Do you have a God?

Me: Well, I do need to believe, so I believe in power, something bigger than me. Sometimes I give it a name of a God that others can relate with. I need belief to cope with the Uncertainty Bugbear.

Tan Tan: 'Power bear' to fight Uncertainty Bugbear'! Pow ...Biff ...biff ...

Me: It's useful to have some part of the *power* inside of me, say in my own talents and skills. In the story about Samson, the strongest man ever, his parents had him believe that all his power was in his long hair. Delilah tricked him and cut off his hair while he slept. When he woke up, he was so heartbroken that though he had no injuries like Hari had, he still could not use his legs and arms.

Tan Tan: A big strong man did not believe in his own muscles?

Me: Belief is carried so deep that reason does not get there easily.

Tan Tan: But everything is connected! Come on Samson, you can do it!

Me: Yes, luckily everything is connected, so reasoning does help in changing fixed belief and attitude. Samson got back his strength through anger.

Tan Tan: Eh? I thought anger is a bad thing!

Me: Emotions come out of the values we hold dear. Suppose Samson carried a value for truthfulness; he would be angered by the trickery through which he was captured. Anger helps to connect us with what we care deeply about. When we understand what we value, we know why we must act and the 'why' will show us how to go about it. Anger woke up Samson's Power Bear and he went biff bang crash!

Tan Tan: When I get angry, I become stronger too! Oh, I think I got it! A value got me angry and anger made me strong, so power really came from my value!

Me: Anger releases extra energy via neurochemicals, but you be careful about what you do with that. Power Bear has to connect with intelligence, and then you can use power sensibly and Power Bear can even be called Courage Bear. The Native American grandfathers say *courage* is a bear. That makes a well-connected bear, deep inside the values box, through belief in your own abilities, through to the top layers of intelligent analysis. Connecting with intelligent systems allows us to have a handle on the subconscious, so it does not go off like a runaway train with no driver, or with a drunken driver.

Tan Tan: This morning when I was feeling left out of the game, the need for belonging was in the driver's seat of my body.

Me: Needs are reckless drivers.

Tan Tan: You're not too good with explaining hope, faith or belief, but I guess you tried hard enough.

Me: Only my rational conscious thinking brain has the luxury of explaining things, and hope lives in the irrational plane. I have respect for it because I have seen it healing the sick and injured from inside when as a doctor all I could do was to provide support.

Tan Tan: That would be a doctor's belief at work along with the nurse's hope.

USS 4
EMOTION

CHAPTER 5

ARE BAD EXPERIENCES GOOD TEACHERS?

As I was entering my study, Tan Tan pounced on me from behind the door with a lusty roar, giving me a nasty fright. After jumping clean out of my skin, I realized that it was only Tan Tan the prankster; it took me a while to steady my fluttering heart, and I can't remember what I had composed in my head as the beginning of this chapter. As I settle down and turn on my computer, my hands are still shaking.

Tan Tan: Are you OK? (he is looking worried now) I'm sorry, I got here before you did so....

Me: I'm alright Tan Tan, just need a few seconds to mop up the fright.

Tan Tan: Can I get you a mop?

Me: [*Smiling*] No no, my neurons will clean up the spilled adrenaline.

Tan Tan: Oh, so we just wait? Okay, I can do that. Where did you spill adrenaline?

Me: It started in the amygdala in the limbic area of the mid-brain. Your sudden movement and yell set off an alarm signal that flashed in three other places, right down to the adrenal glands sitting on top of my kidneys.

Tan Tan: I'm so terribly sorry! I had no idea....

Me: Don't worry Tan Tan, feelings are what make life worthwhile. Imagine if you couldn't distinguish if you like or don't like something! (Right now, I know I don't like Tan Tan.)

Tan Tan: My baby brother knows what he doesn't like already! And lets the whole world know too.

SENSE OF WHAT I LIKE OR DON'T LIKE

The limbic system (Figure 5.1) lies in the deeper layers of the cortex and generates emotions—both pleasant and unpleasant—records memories and triggers motivation. A stimulus to trigger emotion could be something happening now, a recalled event or even imagined situation or an image. An emotionally significant stimulus activates selectively a region within the limbic system that matches that class of emotion, which in turn secretes its own custom neurotransmitter or influences powerful endocrine glands

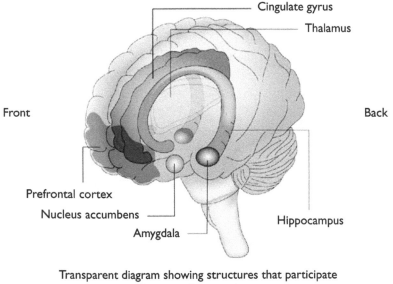

Transparent diagram showing structures that participate in generating emotions

Figure 5.1. Biological Seat of Emotions: Limbic System in the Brain
Source: Goleman (1995)

to secrete related hormones. These chemical messengers create conditions within the body and brain that collectively give rise to the emotion—a sense of what we like or don't like. Any emotion involves the whole body and modifies it.

Emotion modifies the body in the following ways:

- Change in facial expression
- Matching body posture and position
- Change in muscle tone
- Change in blood pressure
- Changes in circulatory system (blushing, paleness, reddening of ears)
- Change in heart rate and respiratory rate
- Changes in digestion
- Changes in immune function/healing

Emotion modifies the brain in the following ways:

- Changes in attention and focus
- Changes in ideation and planning
- Appropriate style of mental processing in response to threat or reward
- Changes in speed of processing

The generation of emotion and its effects on the body and brain lie below the level of conscious thought. Pathways in the mid-brain are swift and can trigger defensive reaction in a fraction of a second (in milliseconds). Actions originating in the reactive zone are guided by ingrained values and fears; they follow a pattern of habit and drill that has been practised enough times to have formed consolidated and efficient nerve circuits for the activity. Nature grants right of way to agile reaction circuits over slow signals from the thinking brain with its innumerable and recursive inter-connections and does so wisely because survival demands speed. But to retain life-saving alacrity, the emotional brain has to compromise on consideration. When emotion takes over command, we call it an 'amygdala hijack' (Goleman 1995; Amygdala—Emotional Centre in the Limbic Mid-brain).

Tan Tan: That's the word I was looking for—'hijack'! It means that the driver's seat of your body has been taken over by emotion. Last time it was the 'need for belonging'.

Me: A hijacker is usually hostile and alien, so the word is not accurate when applied to emotion. In the brain, emotion has a vital role. It is vigilant and quick, and indispensable in emergency. It is the limbic system located deep in the brain that houses the emotional nuclei, and their speed is what comes handy in life and death circumstances.

Emotion in the driver's seat is an undisciplined driver, but not a bad direction finder. I say this because emotions are molecules released into circulation in tune with embedded values or their flip side anti-values (fears), so they are faithful to a principle. Emotions being short-sighted could be service providers to values, like communication services, logistic services, making energy available, sharpening attention and focus, but they are such eager players that they prefer to take over controls. In every team, there are eager members itching to wrest authority from the captain, but it's the responsibility of the captain to retain position and function. Let's see how we can make emotion let go of the steering wheel and brakes.

Signals from all parts of the body including viscera are picked up and relayed to the thinking levels via the insula. When emotional information reaches the conscious 'knowing' region, humans can learn to recognize and name the feeling and deal with it intellectually. It takes only half a second for the insula to deliver the information to the analytical forebrain. If we are trained to pause for half a second before acting upon emotion, the PFC can interrupt a pre-programmed habitual pattern of reaction and replace it with a considered response. Being analytical in nature, the frontal brain can think up an array of possible options and decide which is most suited to the situation. Human intelligence is built on a predictive model. Intelligence, when it gets time, is able to apply consequential thinking and guess the consequences of each option before choosing the best one. The forebrain is responsible for executive functions and can even calm the agitated amygdala (emotional centre) via the orbito-frontal cortex (OFC), to recover physical composure, brain attention and focus. In other words, the half-second pause allows emotional intelligence to be engaged and activated.

Tan Tan: What's that?

Me: Emotional intelligence is the ability to sense our own emotions and to regulate them appropriately, and also sense the feelings of others. This ability allows us to get along with others, work together in teams and exercise leadership in personal and professional spheres.

Tan Tan: Useful! Are you sure the forebrain can do so much in half a second? You just said that it is slow.

Me: Slower than the reactive life-saving mid-brain, but yes, half a second. If you're not getting killed you can take more time and get creative. But at least take half a second to assess what is happening is not going to kill you because brain funk begins to cascade without taking in the details.

Tan Tan: Body freeze for half a second, don't kick, swear or yell— just half a second? Um… okay, I think I can do that—maybe with some practice.

Me: If you can practise the pause, values and cool contemplative intelligence can hang on to the controls and take cues from emotions because emotion has its own simple quick logic (like/don't like). An emotional brain may not be analytically bright, but it's not stupid. It communicates on behalf of non-verbal attributes of values, anti-values (fears) and wisdom, and has the means to regulate energy of enthusiasm and rage. Don't dismiss emotion; consult it like you would a valuable ally. It is well connected within the vast subconscious. Emotion is also the best cheerleader. When we ignore and neglect emotions, we can't find energy required to rise above mediocrity and bid for excellence.

Practising the pause is required because there is a 'use it or lose it' rule for living tissues. Repeated use of a set of nerve cells, fibres and muscles (e.g., in piano practice) helps the participant tissues to grow in strength, improve efficiency and become able to withstand adverse conditions. A novice has to be mindful of new action during early learning, but as proficiency improves, she/he can continue with less attention. A master can perform the practised manoeuvre even under duress. Using emotional intelligence is a brain function (much like solving math problems or riding a bicycle), and opportunities to use its four-component skill sets in everyday situations strengthen the competence by exercising the OFC which calms the emotional centres and is used when we exercise restraint, and the executive PFC that is sometimes called the 'manager of emotion' trains to retain its place in the driver's seat.

Awareness about emotional intelligence and ways of sharpening the bunch of emotional competences (see Figure 5.2) will make you less avoidant of situations you found distressing earlier. You may be able to view annoyances as opportunities to practise anger management and building patience (as I am doing by tolerating Tan Tan in my study). You may become unafraid of facing disappointment and rejection because you will be using the experience to learn the art of balancing ego. Like the learning of balancing a bicycle only comes from practising and practising cycling many times over. Good experiences are always welcome, but most unpleasant experiences are better teachers in the process of self-discovery and development.

EMOTIONAL COMPETENCE

SELF-AWARENESS	SELF-REGULATION
Awareness of feelings/mood Accurate self-assessment Self-confidence Self-worth	Appropriate behavior Adaptability Initiative Motivation Transparency
EMPATHY	RELATIONSHIP MANAGEMENT
Sensitivity to feelings of others Anticipating needs of others Political awareness Systems awareness	Developing others Conflict management Influence Inspiring others Collaboration/teamwork Leadership

Figure 5.2. Emotional Competence
Source: Author

Tan Tan: What are you saying! Bad experiences are good teachers? The bully in the playground who gave me an arm sprain, you're telling me that he is my teacher?

Me: Depends on what you learned from the experience.

Tan Tan: I learned to read his mood and can guess when I need to run away. I can read it in his eyebrows and the way his arms hang by his sides, even when he has his back to me. I think he's being bullied at home, because he looks sad. I felt sad too, and not just because of the pain in my arm.

Me: That's valuable learning! You just brought me to USS 5! You can sense what someone else is feeling!

USS 5

EMPATHY

I was out on the balcony for a while, talking to a client on the phone. When I returned, I found Tan Tan had converted my office into a home theatre. As I surprised him, I saw him wipe away a tear as he watched that the lion cub had discovered that his father was dead. Tan Tan was very embarrassed about his tears this time.

Me: Ahem, can we get on with USS 5?

Tan Tan: Unh hunh, sure, you said it's about sensing what someone else is feeling.

Me: The name is 'empathy', and I think that you have plenty of it already. Useful for a Ninja and a leader.

CHAPTER 6

NINJAS ALSO REQUIRE EMOTIONAL INTELLIGENCE

Tan Tan: I have USS 5 already? Without knowing about it, without training to learn? With no practice?

Me: Well, rats have been found to have empathy (Bartal 2011).

Tan Tan: One rat can know what the other rat is feeling?

Me: A pet can sense the mood of a significant human, although some fellow humans may be found wanting in the empathy department. (Didn't tell Tan Tan then, but most doctors score low on empathy assessment, and that includes me.) This ability to connect wordlessly with other individuals evolved with 'mirror neurons'. These units of social intelligence have been around so long in the evolutionary scale that we don't need training to start using them. We're so good at using mirror neurons that we can do it subconsciously, although we discovered their existence rather accidentally as late as 1992 (Di Pellegrino et al. 1992).

Based on the discovery of mirror neurons, it is now possible to explain the contagiousness of moods: how we share emotions, how we trust, and how we ascribe intentions to others—even read their minds and imagine future consequences of actions we plan.

Tan Tan: Accidental discovery? Explains so much stuff?

Me: Animals (humans included) living in groups develop societies. They live in groups to survive, and in the safety of togetherness, they seek collective well-being, thereby creating socio-cultural homeostasis—a range of behaviours that maintain health and quality of life in societies. Perhaps mirror neurons co-evolved with group living as a basic unit of social intelligence. Mirror neurons are the units of empathy and social intelligence (Goleman 2006).

Tan Tan: Do they look like mirrors?

Me: No, they just look the same as other neurons. A subset of motor neurons that fire in response to the state of another individual inform the brain about how that person feels based on their own function and experience. When you smile at me, I can't help but smile back. And because I smile when I'm happy, I guess that you are feeling something similar. Since you made me smile, it set off the chemistry of a smile, and my body now contains the same mood chemicals as yours.

Studies on the activation of the human brain during the observation of others in pain show that there is a shared location for processing information about pain of others, and for pain directly experienced by self (Bernhardt and Singer 2012).

Due to this sharing of the pain nucleus, watching someone else in pain could be as distressing as being physically hurt in person. The structures involved in the process are the mid-cingulate cortex and the anterior insula.

Empathy is intrinsic, and babies will become as distressed as another without a clue about the cause of distress. Children about two years old who are upset that one of their friends is hurt will try to calm the other by offering their own comforting symbols, even dragging their own mothers to the distressed one. An older child is able to distinguish the distress as 'not mine' showing that it requires some maturity to do so. A natural response to act upon a painful signal and try to alleviate the suffering is triggered both for self and others.

Signals from own (intact) skin and joints are used to mediate the distinction between 'my pain' and 'not my pain'. Mirror neurons deliver signals of pain experienced by another straight to the pain centre of our brain, and then a more complex process inhibits the pain after assurance that it is 'not my pain'.

Lowering of empathy occurs in medical students during the third year (Hojat et al. 2009). This is the time when they are exposed to real patients and encounter suffering in the course of professional training. They learn to damp down the phenomenon of empathy in order to be more effective and stoic enough to conduct interventions while shielding themselves from the experience of vicarious suffering.

Other factors such as group membership (not one of us) and perception of fairness (serves him right) also inhibit empathy, thereby giving rise to hard-heartedness.

Tan Tan: [*Feeling like a pro*] Okay, so we all come equipped with enough mirror neurons to feel pain when others are hurt, but we lose some empathy on the way by figuring out that it's not me and not one of us. These medical students become hard-hearted .... When were you in third year Dr Sen?

Me: Er… umm… (I told you not to let it out that I scored low on empathy. Don't you know that criminals also score poorly on this parameter! [*not said aloud*])

Tan Tan glances at the newspaper. His eyes linger on a gory headline about a communal clash.

Tan Tan: People are born nice, like rats, and then become cruel to each other because of a different way of thinking. Can you do something about this? Humans have to think.

Me: I try to speak to medical students before they get to the third year. The good news is that with awareness, the drop, in empathy observed in the third year, can be minimized. Awareness can help us use our brain better.

Tan Tan: Have your empathy scores improved?

Me: Tan Tan (I am trying to change the subject here), what is non-verbal communication?

Tan Tan: Oh, that's the long conversation mom was having with baby brother! Woke me up with the babble. I was irritated, but they seemed so tuned in. And I know that you are trying to throw me off asking questions about you in the third year!

Me: [*Darn, this kid is sharp*] Not just the sounds we make, Tan Tan, there's so much more to non-verbal communication. Think about all the information you got from the Big Bully from his face and back muscles. Out of all communication between humans, 70 per cent is non-verbal. We could miss so much information if we did not have mirror neurons! Information is power.

> *The most important thing in communication*
> *is hearing what isn't said.*
> —Peter F. Drucker

Social structure and function thrive on a phenomena based on these responsive nerve cells. It is because of them that we are able to anticipate needs and discomfort of others and orient ourselves for providing services efficiently. Having this sense of what others are thinking and how they are thinking can be applied to groups and equips us with organizational and political awareness.

The tendency to protect ourselves from vicarious distress is enforced by the stronger and more basic sense of self; hence, the inhibition of empathy occurs efficiently (as seen in the medical students study) and subconsciously. Life can go on but leaving much to be desired. I have asked many patients (and doctors who have serious illness) knowing that it is essential for a health worker to inhibit empathy in order to be stoic enough to do his/her work efficiently: Would you want a health service provider to score high on empathy or low?

Tan Tan: High, high, very high!

Me: How can that be?

Tan Tan: Talk to them please. Not just doctors—police, architects, drivers, scientists, everyone!

Me: Scientists?

Tan Tan: Yeah, they make bombs.

Me: I am trying Tan Tan. This book is a part of my effort.

ACTIVITIES THAT CAN BE USED TO ENHANCE EMPATHY

The following activities are helpful in enhancing empathy:

1. Listen with full attentiveness.
2. Try to interpret the silence of close friends and take feedback about whether you got it right.
3. Watch a friend return from an errand and try to guess if she/ he was successful. Then check with her.
4. Reflect (mirror) the expression and body configuration of the person you are interacting with at the start of the meeting.
5. Watch a foreign language film without subtitles and read the synopsis later.
6. Use photographs of different facial expressions and poses and try to put captions to them.
7. Spend time with farm animals or pets.
8. Volunteer for childcare or eldercare.
9. Spend time with persons with special needs.
10. During public dealing, make momentary eye contact and watch the effect of your smile on strangers.

Tan Tan: Emotions and empathy and all seem all touchy feely. Not Ninja stuff like martial arts.

Me: Just as your own feelings can hijack your controls, feelings of others are just as strong and agitating. If you cannot stabilize how will you exercise the stoic focus of a Ninja?

Staying in charge of yourself is another way of saying you are Emotionally Intelligent. It is the first of all the multiple intelligences to start working perhaps even before birth. Take a cue from the wisdom of Nature and start by making good use of this, and keep adding competencies on the way to the top.

Tan Tan: Will I need Emotional Intelligence when I am the leader of all Ninja's?

Me: Yes, that's when you will need it all the time.

Tan Tan: Then you have to give me activities to enhance the sense of like and don't like.

Me: You're already very enhanced in that area; what you need to learn through exercise is impulse control. You can make up games around it.

IMPULSE CONTROL

Tan Tan: Statue!

Me: Yes, that's a fun game. Challenge yourself not to laugh at jokes, try not to blink and that game in which we count around a group, say a different word for every multiple of 5.

Tan Tan: Buzz.

Me: The muscle for impulse control (now even I am alluding to the brain as a muscle) can also be exercised by learning to adapt to discomfort, like going camping and living in the forest for a while!

Tan Tan: Last time we went camping we forgot to pack salt! But food still tasted um… okay, and we had a great time!

Me: Here I brought you chocolate chip muffin.

Tan Tan: Mmm… my favorite! Gimme gimme!

Me: Here it is, you can eat it now, but if you wait till the end of this chapter, then you get two muffins.

Tan Tan: Hey that's no fair!

Me: It's up to you.

Tan Tan: I think I'll wait and have two at the end, but it's going to be hard.

What I asked Tan Tan to do just now is called 'delaying gratification'. This was the test given to child subjects of the Marshmallow test conducted by Walter Mischel. The ability of four-year-old children to exercise restraint was tested and the follow-up of these children later in life proved to be a treasure trove of evidence of how well the ability to delay gratification translates into real-life successes. Tan Tan chose to wait for the second muffin, and my respect for this little boy climbed many notches.

I am reminded of the snippet from the epic Mahabharata in which young Karna was trying to stay very still while his Guru Parshuram rested with his head on Karna's lap. Sitting so still is anyway a tough ask for a young lad and that was when a scorpion crawled up and stung Karna on his thigh. Through the excruciating pain and spreading poison, Karna was able to marshal his muscles so as not to disturb the master's slumber. That was an exercise in impulse control.

The Spartan conditions Tan Tan is used to at the monastery are great for building adaptability. Evolution history proves that adaptation to the environment is the single most successful trait for any living being. Living comforts, gadgets and technology that make human life comfortable are all around us. The monks of this order do imbibe modern amenities in everyday living. They use computers in their office and in school and projectors during public addresses, plenty of automation in the kitchen and laundry, but they do continue to segregate the sexes. The debate about whether sex segregation of teens is a good or bad idea still rages. As a coach, I see it as a bad idea since some of my young clients have been unable to exercise balance in behaviour and decision-making once released into the freedom of the real world. Restraint in behaviour is learned by doing and lack of exposure robs humans of opportunity to learn to manage hormonal storms. The young adult is then untrained and vulnerable.

Like adaptability, dynamically balancing between extremes is also a function of internal discipline, which must be learned by practising. It doesn't help if mentors and authorities display extreme behaviours and formulate rules of conduct that are over the top. Parents are the first teachers, mentors and authority figures. Parenting styles play a pivotal role in forming attitudes and outlook (Table 6.1):

1.   *Parenting/leadership style impacts impulse control in children*

Table 6.1. Spectrum of Parenting/Mentoring/Leadership Received

Style	Unpredictable	Dependable
Personality	Ambivalent	Secure base
Guidance	Avoidant	Clear boundaries
Behavioural template	Absent	Sets example
Response to confrontation	Indulgent	Answers questions

Source: Author

Acknowledging the needs vacuums that do not respond to reason because they are hardwired into our biology:

• Need to belong
• Need to connect
• Need to control/certainty
• Need to understand

2.   *Parenting/leadership style impacts thinking styles in children:*

Figure 6.1 shows what consequences the quality of guidance from parents and teachers/mentors has on the development of thinking habits and styles of young people, though all have similar basic needs.

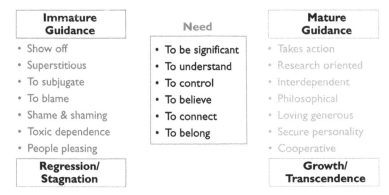

Figure 6.1. Impact of Quality of Guidance
Source: Author

Tan Tan: What is transcendence?

Me: Rising above self.

Tan Tan: The right side of the figure looks good, but my parenting was not dependable. I spend more time at the monastery than at home.

Me: It's the same if you have a mentor or a leader who cares.

Tan Tan: Ah that I have! Looking at the left side of the figure, it seems that sometimes having a parent could be harmful. Do the kids ever get out of stagnation or regression? That means growing backwards, right? Going into the previous century?

Me: Parents often exert their need for control over the choices made by offspring. They have the best intentions but are not necessarily prescribing the best choices because the next generation lives in a different era. I may not know in what way the talents my daughters have can contribute in the future. For them, my knowledge of the world is obsolete. I often restrain my impulse to give unsolicited advice. Let's close this chapter in the spirit of restraint.

Tan Tan: End of chapter! Can I have my second muffin please? I think you stuffed 'impulse control' into the empathy chapter to make my wait for the muffin longer!

USS 6
PAIN AND THREAT PERCEPTION

CHAPTER 7

HURT PEOPLE
'HURT' PEOPLE

T he study is quiet and undisturbed today. I checked and found that Tan Tan isn't here yet, but will certainly turn up. I'm having a sense of imminent disturbance that the will-o'-the-wisp will stir up when he gets here. The prank that startled me threw me off the sequence of the USS discussion, but that doesn't matter as we are still among the structures of the mid-brain, and as we keep reminding ourselves, 'everything is connected'.

We delve into the phenomenon of pain in this chapter and find many levels of connectors that participate in this protective mechanism. The sensors used are often the same sensory nerve endings that deliver the sensations of touch, temperature and pressure. These nerves feature among the five rockstar special senses, but the path taken by signals of pain, mediated by the neurotransmitter named P substance, deviates from the non-painful stimuli within the spinal cord. The processing of nociceptor signals is thus separate from the sense of touch. Nociceptor is the name given to a receptor within a neuron that responds to a dangerous or potentially harmful stimulus.

Apart from the sensors in the skin, there are pain sensors in joints and muscle, and in the coverings of viscera. These signals provide information about dangerous substances, injury and inflammation, and about potential dangers such as the exhaustion of inadequate blood supply and distension of hollow organs and irritation of their linings. This serves to draw conscious attention to the body part and to initiate action aimed at returning to a state of well-being, such as an immediate withdrawal of the part away from the causative factor.

The quick reaction to pain uses short reflex loop pathways that return in a flash from the spinal cord, but the interpretation and processing of pain require the involvement of complex structures of the brain. Pain is interpreted in the anterior cingulate cortex (ACC)—a gyrus that sits curling atop the lateral ventricle of the brain. The activation of this gyrus results in directing attention to the cause of pain, immediate avoidant action and motivation to ensure protection from or destruction of the threatening factor. The ACC is close to the limbic emotional areas, so its activation triggers flooding of emotional neurochemicals, resulting in fear, anger, irritability or anxiety.

On the interpretation of potential harm, a flurry of activity is set off in the autonomous nervous system and simultaneously in the main endocrine axis of the body, named hypothalamic pituitary adrenal axis, HPA axis for short. In simple terms, this is the chemical cascade through which threat translates into stress. The body braces in anticipation of having to deal with emergency conditions by:

- Raising blood pressure
- Increasing blood sugar
- Tensing of muscles
- Directing full attention to focus upon the offending object
- Motivating retaliation or retreat, overriding earlier plans
- Pausing the creative thought process
- Suspending healing processes

Tan Tan bursts through the door and it bangs shut after him.

Me: Uh oh!
Tan Tan: It was an accident! It was an accident!
Me: Whoa, Tan Tan, what happened? Are you hurt?

Tan Tan: The Big Bully is hurt. His head is bleeding. But I didn't mean to kill him! My model airplane is broken now—waaah!

Me: Did he break your model?

Tan Tan: No! He was laughing at it and calling out to other boys to come and make fun of it.

Me: Okay, then what?

Tan Tan: I threw the plane at him, really hard, and a sharp edge got him on the forehead. It wasn't sharp, but became sharp as it broke!

Me: Oh dear! Shall I go and take a look?

Tan Tan: [*Sob*] No they took him to the hospital already, and I had to go to the elder to be scolded [*sob*].

Me: That's why you're late, and I needed you to help me write about *pain and threat perception*! Tell me how did you feel when the big boy was laughing at the model you made so carefully.

Tan Tan: Angry!

Me: Come on, it's easy to give that answer. Think and try to describe what you felt.

Tan Tan: He said my plane is 'ridiculous'.

Me: And you felt?

Tan Tan: Ashamed!

Me: What if the others joined him?

Tan Tan: I would be embarrassed! [*suddenly calming down*] That's not enough reason to get violent I suppose ... but it was an accident!

Me: Neuroscientists have found that the cingulate cortex has a broader function than processing only physical pain. It is now known that social pain, such as experienced due to exclusion/rejection/loss of a loved one, shares the same neural substrate that is used by signals of physical pain (Eisenberger 2012). It is therefore no longer surprising that the emotional and behavioural consequences of physical threat and social disconnection or disgrace are similar, often identically stressful. A similar activation is observed when an expected reward is denied (disappointment).

We know that the pain switch is in the cingulate cortex. I am in physical pain so I hit the switch, and a circuit is already in place to activate a number of physiological autonomic reactions to pain designed for self-preservation via the HPA cascade. Now, Tan Tan comes along, experiencing a socially awful lowering of self-esteem and in desperation hits the same switch; he sets off the exact same full-blown autonomic stress response. Some words we use like 'hurt', 'heartbreak', 'breakdown', 'burnout' and 'breakup' to describe dysfunction originating in interpersonal relationships, and career-oriented relationships give away similar experience of social pain to physical hurt. Loss of a loved one may feel as grievous as bodily harm due to this shared circuitry, with serious clinical consequences like shock.

Survival and well-being in mammals are heavily dependent on social bonding. Infants are completely dependent on caregivers, and later the community shares responsibility for food acquisition, health and predator protection. Due to this profound reliance on society, threats to social connection and social status are interpreted as equally detrimental to survival as physical threats to bodily integrity.

Urgent action (evasive or aggressive) is initiated close to the pain-sensitive area in the cingulate cortex. Persons smarting from painful rejection or lowered self-worth are known to react irrationally and compulsively hurt others or themselves, or persecute to get even. It may be useful to remember that 'hurt people hurt people' (Bowen 2007).

Tan Tan: You mean, it's okay to hit out when someone makes fun of you?

Me: Of course not! This piggyback ride that social discomfort takes on the older mechanism designed for processing physical danger explains why we feel like reacting, but it doesn't justify the physical reaction. Humans have a top-heavy brain packed with intelligence, and we had better learn to distinguish between physical and social threats and respond appropriately!

If the individual perception of social standing is named 'ego' (Sen 2006), then any threat to the maintenance of that status can be considered as 'ego threat', and humans guard their ego boundaries as vigilantly as we safeguard our skin and all that it contains, and then the ego threat perception goes straight to the ACC to set off a cascade of physiological emergency responses and compulsive retaliatory or defensive actions. We pick fights or withdraw into a depressive brooding state. Reaction occurs at a level below conscious rational thought. If we ever take time to think back on how we behaved under ego-threatening conditions, we would probably exclaim, 'What was I thinking!' Contemplation is a slow process of broadening of focus that can only be indulged in relative safety, in the absence of threatening conditions.

Nociception (sense of pain and threat to self) is thus a sense that spans both individual and social realms.

Tan Tan's face is stained with tears, but he's not crying any more. Experience tells me that the look he is wearing precedes a difficult question.

Tan Tan: You're always making excuses for rational thought, saying it is too slow to work in threatening conditions! Isn't that the time when intelligence is most needed?

Me: Yes, the intelligent brain can distinguish between social and physical threats, provided it gets a chance. If you hit first and think later, like today, you will have to answer to the elder. There will be consequences and you will spend a good part of your life in damage control.

Tan Tan: You just told me about the pause yesterday! Intelligence needs half a second to start working.

Me: Lucky you heard about this when you're young. Life will throw you many curved balls and you will get many chances to train your brain to pause and connect. The world is competitive and competition is perceived as threatening. You also have to learn to distinguish between your ideas and identity. The bully was laughing at the model you made, not at you. The brain churns out idea after idea; sometimes your idea will be rejected for someone else's. Let the best idea win.

Tan Tan: A better plane would not have broken!

Me: We could have been on that plane. For society, it works to let the best idea win, and all its members can benefit from the best inventions. Ideas compete with each other, not the humans who conceived them.

Tan Tan: The bully laughs at my name, my hair, the way I talk— all that is me!

Me: Tan Tan, you are not your hair or your name. You are your values and priorities. What you stand up for, what you're willing to die for. Priorities can change and values rearrange themselves, but that's who you are. You can be proud of your values, and feel safe that they will stay with you as long as you maintain self-worth as a safety belt.

Tan Tan: I can be proud of my intelligence?

Me: You can be grateful because it's a gift. Not everyone is blessed with the same abilities or looks, talents or opportunities. When you become aware of your blessings, you must nurture and exercise your talents; use them for the greater good, that you can be proud of.

Tan Tan: I will become the leader of the Ninjas. Then I will be proud!

Me: Status is important to the individual. Leadership is really an inherent need of society. In most species that live in groups, the position of a leader is hardly ever vacant. Members displaying adequate abilities and initiative spontaneously rise to occupy the position. There may be more than one member qualified for the position, and different members may take the lead for different purposes. Closely matched candidates may have to compete for the spot. Occasionally they fight, and it may result in death. Competition is historically interpreted by the brain as life-threatening and stressful.

Tan Tan: Great warriors killing each other inside the same group? What a waste!

Me: To avoid a fatal battle, the contenders for higher spots on the hierarchy indulge in showing off their abilities so the competitors get the message and refrain from challenging the alpha individual. Humans tend to show off their intelligence to intimidate competitors. Showcasing brilliance involves an investment of energy in flaunting one's opinions and analysis. It can feel awful if someone else reveals a flaw in the argument. Having invested in showmanship, it becomes incumbent on the individual to zealously guard credibility. This is called intellectual sparring and can get messy. We find 'The Need to be Right Syndrome' and 'Knights of the Last Word', as common afflictions of the times.

Tan Tan: You're way behind the times! We show off hi-tech gadgets.

Me: Status symbols are displays that serve a similar purpose of staying visibly one step ahead of others and pre-empting the need to joust and prove one's worth.

Tan Tan: Less bloodshed?

Me: The displays, whether through winning arguments, greater wealth, powerful connections or sexual conquests all require investment of energy, time and money. These could have been put to good use if people felt secure enough to refrain from competitive displays.

Tan Tan has crawled under the desk. He has a finger on his lips to tell me not to speak.

Me: Now what?

Tan Tan: The bully is back with a bandage on. Now, I have to walk back to class through the kitchen and behind the pumpkin patch.

Me: That way is almost four times the distance! You will waste time and energy and get late for class!

Tan Tan: You know 'hurt people hurt people'. He will certainly get back at me!

Me: You could apologize? You didn't mean to draw blood. He is really injured and can do with some kindness to help him heal.

Tan Tan: Like walk up and talk with him?

Me: Why not? Acknowledged people respond better than hurt people.

Tan Tan: He's probably in pain, so am I. Why do I have to be the one to apologize? [*Sulk*]

Me: Pain is a blessing, but we have misunderstood its message. Because discomfort feels bad, we regard it as a bad thing to be avoided at all cost. Giving pain nuisance value alone is erroneous, and this error is causing us anxiety, as discomfort is everywhere.

Tan Tan: Pain feels really bad. How can you say that it's a blessing?

Me: Remember, it was designed for physical protection. If you hurt your arm, it must feel bad when you move it. That will force you to not move it about, until it gets a chance to heal. Inadvertent movement could happen when you are pre-occupied, and the acute unpleasantness of the sensation brings your attention back to the injured part so you take better care of it. The anxiety hormone generated by pain makes sure that your attention hovers around the injury and makes you hypervigilant to prevent further injury. Perhaps that is why you don't want to come face to face with Big Bully again; you want to avoid the conditions that caused you discomfort.

Tan Tan: I got time to think now, so my intelligence knows that my pain is social and bully is physically hurt. He needs to go to the room and rest, but I can go to class. It will still be difficult to pay attention, though.

Me: Yes, attention is finite. When pre-occupied, only the remainder of attention is available for performing tasks. Just like the physical, social pain also steals from the bandwidth of attention and refuses to allow an individual to function at full potential. Hurt, heartbreak, rejection and grief take time, but do eventually heal well enough to allow the person to reclaim capacity for joyous creativity and productivity. But some people continue to harbour the pain, the sadness and anger that goes with pain, way past the time required to heal.

Tan Tan: Is two years a long time? Dad refused to buy me a bicycle and I have to walk to school. I am angry at him still.

Me: Two years is long. We don't take that long to mourn the loss of a loved one. If someone derived benefit from having been injured, she/he may not be in a hurry to heal or rehabilitate. The victim then prolongs the pain through the mechanism of *resentment*.

Tan Tan: You're talking weird now. Whoever gets benefit from being hurt?

Me: Being victim is one of the ways of being. Some people like being that way!

Tan Tan: Like how can I start liking being a victim?

Me: By having someone to blame. That way we can feel less responsible; it is easier than having to take responsibility for the present situation.

In comparison to the person we hold responsible for our pain, we feel like a better person. That feels doubly good. Being the aggrieved person, I can get a lot of attention and social traction.

Within relationships, victim games are quite popular. Purposefully recalling past hurts and picking at and displaying wounds works as a repeated reminder to the others that they did not live up to your expectations. I can even use these reminders as punishment to people who I know will feel my pain.

Tan Tan: But someone who feels your pain would be rather close to you. Why would you punish someone who cares for you?

Me: Ah! Such a powerful feeling! To be holding a grudge, I can use it to make you feel my pain and also make you feel guilty for being the cause of that pain, or somehow complicit, like not being around to save me!

Tan Tan: I'm really feeling guilty about making bully bleed. I'm a good boy, not a violent one.

Me: Yes, had you been one with a nasty disposition, you probably wouldn't feel guilty, so knowing you're a good person, reminding you repeatedly, I can make you suffer guilt a hundred times for one incident. That's a powerful manipulative position. I wouldn't want to move from there in a hurry, especially if the incident proved what I presumed. It feeds my need to be right and to be one up on you.

Tan Tan: Stay cruel means 'victim'!

Me: Stay indignant and unforgiving because you have proved that you don't even deserve forgiveness. Perhaps you want to be forgiven, in which case I can make you jump through hoops and obey my commands dangling the carrot of forgiveness before you.

Tan Tan: Suppose the victim does forgive, then the game is over?

Me: Ending the game is difficult because I have started enjoying the privileges of being victim. Moving out of this comfortable position, where I was not feeling responsible for any part of the mess would mean that I begin to take responsibility for at least some part of how things are and make the effort required to change my pattern of thinking. I would suddenly find free mindspace that I would be obliged to put to good use!

Tan Tan: Where does the free mindspace come from?

Me: Resentful thoughts occupy space and have to be recycled repeatedly in order to maintain victimhood. This pre-occupation consumes energy and, apart from occupying mindspace, it produces the neurotransmitter hormones of feel-bad which have the attention capturing ability. All these resources, space, energy and attention are limited, and only the leftover resources can be applied to tasks.

Tan Tan: I can study better if I forgive the bully?

Me: And Dad.

The feel-bad neurotransmitters manufactured by resentment don't allow people to feel joy in full measure. The feel-good chemistry is good for analytical and creative brain work. Try forgiving once and tell me how that feels.

Tan Tan: How does one do that? Do I write an 'I Forgive You' card?

Me: No no, he doesn't need to know how you feel. It's all inside of you. If you really like to write, then write the answer to the question: What did I learn from the disappointing incident?

> *Nothing ever goes away until it teaches us*
> *what we need to know.*
>
> —Ani Pema Chödrön

Only we have power over our thoughts. Work towards stopping the thoughts, reversing the feel-bad and gradually assuring yourself that you don't need the black cloud of resentment in your brain any longer; you can do all that right here, by yourself. To help the process you can pay attention to your breathing. Close your eyes and imagine a black cloud inside your head that is sailing away and allowing the light in.

Tan Tan closes his eyes, breathes slowly and deeply, then settles to more normal breathing, opens his eyes just a bit and holds out his arms.

Tan Tan: I let the feel-bad float away. I feel light! Not the light from the sun, but light like a feather—floating light!

He is smiling and gliding around the room, suddenly he hugs my knees.

Tan Tan: Thank you, thank you! This feels so good! I will do much better at kung fu today!

I pat him affectionately and get infected by the innocent joy of his expression.

Me: So when pain comes along, know that its work is to protect you and to protect your self-esteem. Then you let it hang around only as long as needed to heal the hurt, and learn some lessons from the injury or the failure, then you make it leave.

Tan Tan: Or it will stay on and on and make you feel heavy like you're carrying around a big sack of rotten potatoes.

Me: Pain is so clingy that we must check if it has really cleared out with all its baggage, and then we can get on with our lives wholeheartedly at full capacity.

Tan Tan: Could leave some of the stinking trash hidden in some corner? How would I know?

Me: You could learn to use your introspection muscle.

USS 7
INTEROCEPTION

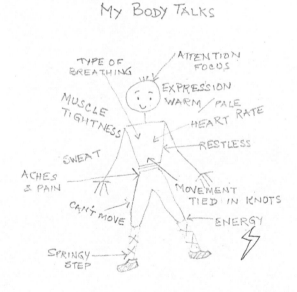

My Body Talks

CHAPTER 8

STOMACH SPEAKS LOUDER WHEN I'M AFRAID

Tan Tan: Introspection means seeing inside? You got the spelling all wrong on the chapter title.

Me: Interoception is correct. It means perceiving information from inner organs and processes of your own body.

Tan Tan: Huh? Why would I want to know?

Me: Because this perception is useful during introspection and getting to know yourself.

Tan Tan: Like how far down in my intestines has my hamburger gone? That doesn't tell me much about me!

Me: USS 7—'Interoception' or 'perception of what's happening on the inside'—works through signals the brain receives from the visceral organs to create a perception of the physiological 'condition' of the body (Craig 2003). This information contributes to a sense of well-being and brings to awareness essentially subconscious processes of emotion and mood via their rather significant influence of internal organs. Research in the area of interoception has only become possible after the advent of functional imaging. Individual variations occur in the ability to sense visceral information (e.g., heartbeat), though people can learn to receive and process these low-volume inputs over time. The messages we get from the gut are of tightening, distension and excessive movement.

Tan Tan: Excessive movement is familiar.

Me: We get messages from every muscle about tone, fatigue and inadequate blood supply. The heart is a muscle too, and it may convey signals about lowered blood supply, but to the conscious brain that message is interpreted as pain in the inner side of the left arm.

Tan Tan: That's too fuzzy. Not a very sensible sense.

Me: It's extremely valuable once you learn to make use of it. Visceral sense (interoception) contributes to 'gut feeling' and forms the mechanism by which we get in touch with (become conscious about) information filed in the non-verbal areas like basal ganglia which contains experience data like 'what works and what doesn't'.

Detection of stirring in the visceral domain can be informative about deeply ingrained values and fears, even prejudice and stereotypes that we harbour but don't really know about because they were unquestioningly imbibed through childhood.

Tan Tan: My stomach does talk, but not all the time! I think my stomach was the one telling me to take the longer pumpkin patch route to avoid the bully. Should I listen to my gut or not?

Me: Must listen. Listen does not mean that you have to obey. Listen to your gut, and then use intelligence to decide whether to act on the hunch or put it away, or just check and double check the line of action that intelligence prescribes. The tightness in your stomach tells you to take the safer but longer route, and intelligence says that meeting the bully would give you an opportunity to apologize and empathize with him, so why waste energy on avoiding him. Check if the advantage of improving your relationship with a person is higher than the benefit from avoiding an awkward meeting. Choose an action based on that priority rating, not on fear alone.

Tan Tan: My teacher says choose the path that brings people closer, to work together harmoniously, and, to avoid actions that push people away from each other.

Me: The emotional state of fear is characterized by a strong set of physiological markers such as accelerated heart rate, high blood pressure, lowering of skin temperature due to the constriction of surface capillaries and sweating. It is also associated with strong influence on the gut that maybe described as 'gut-wrenching' sensation. Apart from the perceptible cramping, nausea or dry mouth, there are other effects the emotions of fear and anxiety wield on the extensive length of the gastro-intestinal tract which may not manifest immediately but may occur later in the form of disturbances of bowel movement, acidity, ulceration and even lowered capacity to fight infections. The relationship between the gut and the brain is extensive and it works both ways. Gut disorders can be as much the cause of clinical depression, anxiety disorders and behavioural conditions as the other way around. This rich two-way connectivity forms the neural infrastructure for the 'ultra special gut sense'.

Tan Tan: My stomach speaks louder when I'm afraid. Other times, I can't hear it.

Me: Fear signals are privileged with right of way because it signals emergency situations that demand lightning fast action. Other emotions such as trust, happiness, achievement and anxiety also wield their influence on the gut and cardiovascular system. These signals may not be 'loud', but they wield significant influence. The physical condition of the viscera is transmitted to the intelligent levels of the brain through interoceptive pathways.

For incoming signals from viscera to reach the conscious levels of the neocortex, they have to pass through the tracts of the insula (a part of the brain tucked beneath the temporal lobe cortex). This brain lobule integrates sensations of the body state with high-level cognition. Researchers at OptiBrain Center of University of California, San Diego, studied the insula of ace athletes (Lovero et al. 2009). They observe that the ability to anticipate the body's requirements for the next action and to calculate the energy required to achieve it lies with the insula. It is closely linked with the function of the ACC which participates in decision-making and initiates corrective action in line with the anticipation. Together they make a winning team. Having strength merely does not improve performance. The efficient use of energy, anticipation of possible deviations and corrective timely adjustments all rely on the insula for execution. Interestingly, brain tissue performance is linked to its bulk. People who train physically at activities requiring an eye–hand coordination, such as ball games and racket sports, have bigger insulae.

Tan Tan: Maybe David's insula was bigger than that of Goliath? David spent a lot of time practising, using the sling shot like me at the mango tree. It needs concentration.

Me: Holding on to awareness of limbs and muscles called 'mindfulness' training and invoking positive emotion called 'compassion meditation' have been shown to result in insula enlargement (Davidson et al. 2003).

The importance of interoception lies in connecting the conscious and the subconscious levels of the brain—a communication path that opens up the wealth of the subconscious for the thinking levels to access, consult, refresh and reset. Information about mood and emotion is obtained by routing signals from changes to visceral states, induced by neurotransmitters of emotion, to conscious levels via the insula. Lifted thus into the conscious zone, the recognition of the emotion becomes possible. The detected state is now amenable to regulation through calming the influence of the PFC (emotional manager) exerted via the OFC back to the amygdala where emotions are generated.

Tan Tan: What about becoming conscious about how someone else is feeling?

Me: Certainly, empathy is intrinsic at the level of mirror neurons, but becoming aware and conscious of how others are feeling happens via the insula. Remember that the contagiousness of emotions of others actually makes us recreate their emotion within our bodies via chemical mediators. These molecules will influence our internal organs, and their changes are conveyed to the conscious brain through the same interoceptive pathways that we use for own emotions. This makes your pain as distressing as my own and triggers appropriate action to help or calm another person! Just feeling someone else's pain is never enough; one has to act to communicate the concern.

Tan Tan: Is your insula working good?

Me: I think so. Why do you ask?

Tan Tan: There is this problem with doctors losing empathy as students in the third year that you spoke about....

Me: I'm practising mindfulness meditation to reverse that damage. I think I'm back to original settings. Tan Tan, are you breathing?

Tan Tan: No.

Me: No?

Tan Tan: No... Yes! Of course, I am breathing.

Me: Now, take a few conscious and long breaths. That's mindful breathing. Now, become mindful about how your clothes feel on your skin.

Tan Tan: Hunh? My clothes don't feel—oh but they do!

Me: Can you feel the weight of your body on the chair? Feel the chair at the back of your thighs. Cup both hands over your ears. What do you hear?

Tan Tan: Roaring! Is that the sea?

Me: It's only your blood rushing in your arteries.

Tan Tan: Wow! This is fun! What's this game called?

Me: Mindfulness.

Tan Tan: It's easy!

Me: Do it whenever you can. Walk with conscious awareness about your limbs, how they move, where they bend. The more you do, the more practice your insula gets. You get better at interoception.

Tan Tan: I'm not bad at catching fear signals. Can I turn up the volume of happy feelings?

Me: Fear can hijack attention—it has to, because whatever one is alarmed by can be life-threatening, but happy feelings free up attention, so you can choose what to do with the extra attention it makes available. It is natural to get busy doing something, like solving the problems of the world, and overlook the way your body is feeling while feeling good.

Tan Tan: Why bother looking inwards when things are going great? Everything is supposed to go well, isn't it?

Me: No, it is not! How did you get that notion?

Tan Tan: Oh?

Me: Humans work hard to create systems that work well, but things do go wrong. I suppose you also take for granted that your body and all its organ systems will work perfectly forever.

Tan Tan: It won't?

Me: You must know, that is a silly question.

Tan Tan: Yes, deep down I do know. But I don't want to know.

Me: When things are going right, we must acknowledge it by feeling good.

Tan Tan: I only know how to feel anger. I can make me angry by just remembering what the bully did.

Me: Become familiar with happy feelings in your body, and then you'll be able to bring on the feel-good when you want to.

Happy feelings free up attention; you can direct some of it to your gut and muscles and check on how they are feeling using the interoceptive pathways. To begin, you can count your blessings.

Tan Tan: What are my blessings?

Me: You're smart enough to tell.

Tan Tan: I'm smart.

Me: That's a blessing. You had asked if you can be proud of your intelligence. If you remember that it is a gift because everyone is not granted the same amount or type of intelligence, then you may feel slightly different from proud.

Tan Tan: Grateful?

Me: Make a list of everything you have to be grateful about. Watch how your breath becomes slower and your neck muscles relax. Allow the grateful feeling to trickle into your limbs, right down to your toes. Wiggle them around, even with shoes on. The longer you can keep gratefulness sloshing around in your muscles, the more nourishment your creative thinking brain is receiving.

Tan Tan: Nice! My neck is loose and my head is falling over backwards! How did I do that? I made myself feel grateful!

Me: Remember, the path is two-way: subconscious to conscious and conscious to subconscious. After some practice the contented feeling becomes familiar, and you can slip into that condition at will and recognize it easily when it happens spontaneously. You will also recognize when you fail to reach the familiar contentment you have practised at leisure. That will inform you about the level of stress in your body. Chronic stress can become insidious and unseen, and it slowly corrodes health, so it's useful to have a way of checking on your internal environment.

I rather enjoy solving problems and correcting what is wrong in the world. It gives me a sense of achievement which is chemically an endogenous kick of dopamine, which is heady and addictive. So I chased problems and wallowed in the euphoria of achievement I received from solving them. For a while I felt really important and indispensable. I was addicted to challenge. I worked without vacation and could not find time to attend academic updates. I made a lot of money, but had no time to enjoy myself.

Tan Tan: That sounds stressful!

Me: Then my heart rate and rhythm gave out warning signals that showed up in my annual health check results.

Tan Tan: You burned out?

Me: I was addicted to stress and way behind in academic growth. When I stopped to check, I found that my knowledge and skills were outdated. I was out of touch with me.

Tan Tan: Your values and what you stand up for?

Me: Wisdom, the 'deep down I do know' guy. It sits about as deep in the brain as values. Too deep to speak in words. Which is why it speaks through the interoception networks and I wasn't listening. Not being able to access wisdom, I was making poor decisions and getting more stressed.

Tan Tan: My network is only tuned to fear and anger signals. I will practise listening to grateful messages from today. How do I talk with the wisdom guy?

Me: You don't talk to wisdom. You just listen. But I learned that the hard way. In those days, I used my interoceptive apparatus for chattering away with my thoughts. I would guess what others are thinking and continuously make moral judgements about how others should behave. I had a rating system through which I would parade people on a catwalk in my head and quickly rate and label them. Somehow rating others upset my own ratings and that made me shaky, so another conversation would start in parallel about whether I am good enough. So many conversations inside that I missed what people around me were saying! In such a noisy head, I could not hear wisdom at all.

Tan Tan: Does it know a lot?

Me: It knows what works and what doesn't. My own personal consultant.

Tan Tan: Will wisdom help me play better chess?

Me: I didn't know you play chess.

Tan Tan: I don't.

Me: Strategic thinking and applying 'what if' scenarios is a function of the very new cortex way up here, just behind the forehead. Chess, or any other competence, is not pre-installed. The brain learns by doing. Wisdom is less cluttered than the rest of your brain because it only sponges up the lessons of life, not the processes or calculations. It just knows the essence.

Tan Tan: Clever! How did wisdom get there? Is it pre-installed like mirror neurons and pathways?

Me: Wisdom grows with experience. That is what I was missing out. I had a lot of experience. The conscious brain stored the data. Essential lessons steeped into the deeper layers to generate intuitive responses. This wealth of codified information derived from the essence of experience was eluding me, not being able to tune in when required.

Tan Tan: How to 'tune in' if it has no words?

Me: Wisdom speaks through emotions, and all the effects emotions have on the organs you can hear through interoception, such as your heartbeat and knotting up of intestines, discomfort of acids and indigestion, tightness of muscles.

Tan Tan: To listen to all that I can't have noisy wordy conversations with thoughts! Shshh...

Me: Wisdom lives close to where values are stored, so it can tell you if your plans are in line with what you regard as worthy. It tells you if what you're doing will make you proud of yourself or ashamed. To let you know that you're in line and upholding your truest values, it presents you with a burst of high energy. If you're betraying your values, it turns your limbs into lead and you find it hard to move them.

Tan Tan: I know that feeling!

Me: To train yourself to access wisdom become familiar with a range of feelings to use as information. Try to name the feelings. When you do that, you bring the feeling up to the level of word processing, the conscious new cortex, a place where one feels more in charge of things, the workplace of executive functions.

Tan Tan: I get to know the feelings, name them, and then because I know them, I can deal with them? I am using conscious emotional intelligence as an interpreter of wordless wisdom.

Me: Self-awareness enables self-regulation. Familiarity with the full range of emotions also equips you to recognize what someone else is feeling. Suppose I have never felt disappointed or frustrated before. The first-time exposure to that emotion can be completely unsettling because I have never learned how to deal with it, nor can I recognize that you are in trouble. Do you remember the story of Prince Siddhartha?

Shuddhodana was the king of Kapilavastu and the father of Prince Siddhartha. Being a loving and responsible father, the king tried to shield the prince from feeling bad, probably due to love for his heir. From a position of power, he may have believed that he could control the workings of the mind.

Prince Siddhartha wanted to go away and live in the forest to seek the path to end misery of all of humanity. On getting wind of Siddhartha's interests, Shuddhodana, like a good wealthy father, tried everything to keep the prince in the palace. He insisted on the prince taking a wife and laid out the ultimate pleasures and luxuries available to a young man, with instructions to the guards to watch out and prevent his renouncement. But Siddhartha felt incomplete and directionless. He had questions and was hungry for answers, not for empty indulgence. He left with a trusted friend Channa on a strong horse and sped away deep into a forest, looking for surroundings conducive to contemplation. He called out to a hunter and begged him to exchange clothes. He used his well-worn sword for the last time to cut off his long and growing hair and then sent Channa back to the king with the horse and princely jewels.

Siddhartha was brave to stay back alone in the wilderness, exposed, unguarded and unprovided. He meditated deeply, learned to tame the demons of the psyche and fend off predators of the forest. He sought out the suffering of humans in order to understand and alleviate their misery. His quest led him to the answers he was seeking and fulfilment of purpose. They say that he achieved 'enlightenment'.

Tan Tan: Much more learning than he may have found in the comfort of the palace. He became the Buddha. A braver and greater leader than his father could have dreamed!

Me: The king valued his son's comfort, but the prince valued the comfort of all humans. As a mentor the king may have recognized immense potential in the prince and spent a lot of time and energy, even money in selectively depriving the prince from experiencing unpleasant sensations. Siddhartha perceived gaps in his upbringing as he was shielded from experiencing and knowing hardship. We all need to feel and understand the full swathe of the emotional spectrum. Having the ability to 'feel' is a precious privilege, and we cannot imagine life without feelings.

Tan Tan: Yeah what would that be like?

Me: Empty.

Tan Tan: Like—not quite alive? Then why would I do what I do?

Me: A wholesome life is one which provides opportunities for all sorts of experience and feelings, leading to complete all-round development. Blocking of emotions will come in the way of internal communication between conscious and subconscious processes and deprive us of the vocabulary we use to access to our own wisdom.

Tan Tan: Being a father or a king isn't enough to become wise.

Me: Shuddhodana's fears pushed him to control his son's experience of life and that pushed his son away.

Tan Tan: Even a king feels fear?

Me: Often we use the word 'fears' to describe what we do not want to come about. We have to refer to this concept frequently, so it wouldn't do to have one word describing an emotional state and the same word for an abstract condition that we would wish to avoid. So, let us agree to use the term 'anti-value' for the latter. Take the example of the *value of truth*. A person who holds truth in high regard will have an anti-value 'dishonesty' or 'falsehood', and a person who values peace will harbour the anti-value 'conflict'. When we detect an anti-value close by, we are motivated to take evasive action or express displeasure through emotional states such as anger or fear. If you don't know what your values or anti-values are, you can find out by checking on what makes you angry or upset.

Instead of trying to block unpleasant feeling, we need to use the information they are trying to convey. The acuteness of discomfort the bad feelings bring on tends to make us avoidant. We develop an anti-value for discomfort.

Tan Tan: You mean a value for comfort? I like comfort.

Me: High regard given to anti-values might create roadblocks on the path to our dreams.

Tan Tan: Ninja dreams or scary dreams?

Me: Which dream do you dream while you're awake?

Tan Tan: Ninja dream. In my awake dream, I am the leader of all Ninjas.

Me: That's the one, the dream you hold when you're awake, you want to follow, and don't let the fear of discomfort get in your way. The feeling of well-being and feeling of discomfort are all delivered to the conscious level through Interoceptive pathways. Keep up the practices that exercise these channels, as the information they carry is much more than comfort, satiation, hunger and concern. They make us powerful through access to essential knowing of wisdom and intuitiveness.

USS 8
POSITION AND BALANCE

USS 9
SENSE OF PASSAGE
OF TIME

USS 10
SENSE OF PROPORTION

USS 11
SENSE OF FAIRNESS

CHAPTER 9

ISN'T IT EXHAUSTING TO BE A LEADER?

The distracting element (Tan Tan) in my study is practising handstands and the crow pose, and I am practising tolerance and restraint. Watching the wiry young person teetering supported only on his palms, I see USS 8 in action, the 'Sense of Position and Balance', also called 'Proprioception'.

This type of perception informs Tan Tan about how his limbs are arranged with respect to the surface of the earth. His brain processes this input efficiently and sends reflex messages to the muscle to contract or relax appropriately in order to maintain stability or to correct the posture.

USS 8 is rather close to the special sense of hearing, though the part of the ear apparatus being used to detect head position—tilting, rotation, acceleration and deceleration—is the less glamorous inner ear with its vestibular apparatus.

The brain needs inputs from the body to know the relative positions of its parts and the strength of muscle power being used even by the vocal chords. Such information, conscious or otherwise, is required when we walk in complete darkness, close both eyes and touch our nose to prove to a policeman that we are sober, to hold an infant without hurting it. The use of this sense becomes quite complex while playing a musical instrument and modulating the voice at the same time. The fact that we do all this effortlessly shows that an efficient signalling system exists between the brain

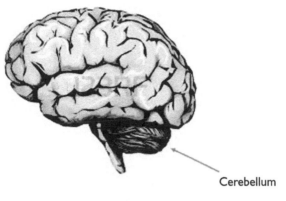

Cerebellum

SIDE VIEW

Located at back of the head, below the level of a cap

Figure 9.1. Side View of the Brain

Source: https://www.123rf.com/photo_45668620_human-brain-and-cerebellum.html

and the limbs via the spinal cord. The cerebellum (Figure 9.1) participates by coordinating the various muscles and the insula in anticipating the next move. Muscle tone and position sense all combine to produce kinaesthesia, a sense of body position movement and poise.

I reluctantly admit that Tan Tan is rather graceful as he does a variation of the crow pose and swings both feet forward with ballet pointed toes.

Kinaesthesia is mostly subconscious but can be brought to the level of conscious awareness. When body movement is conducted with awareness, the action becomes 'mindful'. Movement and posture can thus be converted into a meditative practice as in yoga, tai chi, classical dance forms, playing musical instruments and sport. Mindful motion is a method to get a handle on muscle tone regulation, which is close to physiological processes that influence health, healing and neural well-being which contributes to the executive function.

Using mindful breathing (Pranayama), we can slow it down. Since the rate of respiration and the rate at which the heart beats have a relationship, a slower breath works to slow the heart rate. If you practise breath control, which is a muscular activity, when you are at ease, you learn to do it well enough to repeat while under duress. The practice can help us stabilize quickly after acute stress and recover stamina in situations of fatigue by purposely slowing down the breathing and correspondingly the heart rate.

Conducting movements with awareness routes the signals through the insula. I walk from the office to the dining room every day and pay no attention to the process. If I repeat the same walk with mindfulness, attentive to each muscle and joint in my legs and conscious of the way my arms swing and provide balance to the trunk, I receive the extra benefit of flexing my insula. Bit by bit I develop a stronger and more efficient insula.

Till recently this small lobe tucked away behind the temporal lobe of the brain was overlooked and underrated. Today, we have enough evidence that makes us sit up and take notice of the insula and even respect this diminutive lobe.

The insula integrates mind and body.

Tan Tan: That's USS 7, isn't it? Why did you go back to the insula? We're talking 8 now.

Me: Because the insula has many functions, and neuroscientists are still finding out what more it can do. This is where you find self-confidence.

Tan Tan: That sounds relevant to a Ninja. Go on!

Me: Primordial emotions are generated in the limbic system in the mid-brain, but the complex emotions that are generated through social interactions seem to be produced in the insula, such as embarrassment, resentment, guilt, trust, distrust and humiliation.

Tan Tan: What about love?

Me: That too. Love, hate, pride, empathy, compassion, disgust, contempt, all are here in this little power lobe. Its ability to integrate empathy and muscle coordination gives us the finesse to be gentle, say while handling a baby.

The integrative function of the insula enables us to anticipate what to expect in the next moment. A Ninja and a sportsperson, and actually everybody, need a lot of that competence. The insula can also anticipate how you or someone else may feel if an imagined event occurs.

Tan Tan: Cool! When I play cricket, and am waiting for the bowler, a strong insula will come in handy.

Me: Sportspeople have well-developed insulae as they put in many hours of practice.

Tan Tan: I don't count hours when I'm playing.

Me: Intensely emotional moments can affect our sense of time. Once in a while we feel that time stood still through a certain experience, and that may be happening in the insula, a crossroad of sense of time and desire. Lots happening here!

Tan Tan: Sense of time?

Me: Sense of passage of time. That's USS 9 'Chronoception'.

Tan Tan: Insula does that sense too?

Me: Only the emotional alteration of time. There are other nuclei in the brain that sense the passage of time: suprachiasmatic nucleus, basal ganglia, cerebellum and cerebral cortex.

The phenomenon of jet lag indicates that the body senses night and day which is known as the circadian rhythm. A dedicated nucleus in the brain (suprachiasmatic nucleus) keeps track of night and day and regulates a host of hormone rhythms to alter alertness, sleep, body temperature, digestive activity and immune function. A more diffuse system of neurons involving the cerebral cortex, cerebellum and basal ganglia keeps track of shorter ranges of passage of time (Harrington et al. 2002).

Tan Tan: Perhaps the eye sees if it's day or night. Then this goes to the 'special senses' list.

Me: In the retina, there are some ganglion cells that contain melanopsin. When humans travel across time zones, they reset their system by retraining these ganglion cells. But that is only sense of day or night, not the passing of time.

Tan Tan: Maybe there's a clock or a crystal?

Me: Nerve signals travel through a process of depolarization and repolarization of the cell membrane. Every nerve has an inherent rhythm of readiness for action alternating with spells of a refractory state. During the inactive phase, it does not allow any signal to generate. The interaction between groups of neurons depends on phase relations between their inherent rhythmic activities. Somewhat like a skipping rope held by someone else, and you have to jump only when it hits the ground, the nerve will only allow the signal that arrives when it is ready (repolarized). The alternating nature of readiness and block provides inherent rhythm.

Tan Tan: As a Ninja, I will move quickly and travel far. Do I need to train for USS 9?

Me: You may need to train at timing. The efficiency of the brain as a whole is a function of connectedness between regions and synchrony between the two hemispheres. Brain timing can be improved by engaging in activities that involve synchronized movements of both sides of the body. The phenomenon has obvious implications in dance, percussion, music and sport.

Tan Tan: My kind of stuff?

Me: Everything is connected in the brain, as you are so fond of pointing out, but the different parts need to be in phase and in rhythm. Basic educational exercises prepare a brain for ideation. Different circuits are primed for action separately. The patterns of connection in each brain make it unique, expanding its networks and computing ability. Rhythmicity of signal gateways adds a dimension of timing to training of the brain for the generation of creative thought.

Tan Tan: I don't understand.

Me: It means that learn all your math tables and derivations. The boring drill at PT is setting the timing of firing of defined circuits, so the big network of intelligence can integrate the various rhythms and get creative.

Tan Tan: Practise, practise, practise.

Me: Synchronicity results in graceful movement. USSs 8 and 9—Sense of Position, Balance and Passage of Time—together result in awesome grace, and that sits well on a leader's chair.

Tan Tan: Amazing, Ninja like grace!

Practise synchronous movements with others; it can begin as fun activity like mimicry, but being good at matching other people's movements is a socially useful ability. Try falling into step with someone while walking, enter a seated group by sitting at the same level and copying their pose, muscle tone, even facial expression. This activity is called mirroring. Subconscious mirror neuron function detects synchrony and initiates social bonding.

An interesting application of the sense of time and timing is in humour and clowning, where pausing for a deliberate moment can be very effective in riveting audience attention and enlarging the element of surprise.

Tan Tan: I just got a new idea for a prank to play in class! Element of surprise!

Me: I hope you won't play a prank on someone with a weak heart like you did with me!

Tan Tan: On the pompous overinflated class monitor. He thinks that he is the most important person on earth.

PERCEPTION OF SIGNIFICANCE

Me: What does Tan Tan think about how important he is to the world?

Tan Tan: Umm…

Me: How does anyone know where we stand with respect to the rest of the world?

Tan Tan: I look at other people and see if they are better or if I am, and ask an elder if there is any confusion.

Me: That certainly is one way to receive an external perception of
self. The very first method we use when we are very young is
by observing other individuals' through use of mirror neurons
(Ramachandran 2010) to sense their acceptance and trust
through their expressions and reactions.

My parents love me and give me a lot of attention that makes me
feel I am worthy. I am dependent on them to increase or lower my
sense of worth. A baby crying for a feed or for a change of diaper,
if allowed to cry till many other tasks are taken care of by his
caregivers, gets the impression that she/he is not as important as the
other chores. In case a child is under the care of inconsistent adults,
the child calls for attention, but does not receive the same response
and concern, so she/he may be confused about where she/he
stands with respect to other concerns of the world. This sketchy
information is obtained from intrinsic working of mirror neurons
that also convey expectations held by significant adults through
body language (continuing the 'Pygmalion Effect' discussed in
Chapter 4). We can infer that depending upon others' perception
in order to build assessment about one's own significance puts one
at risk of receiving a misguided or biased perspective about self.
This mechanism is not adequate for a grown person.

USS 1 the primitive 'Sense of Self' places an individual plumb
in the centre of the universe. This (I am the centre of the Universe)
is the first delusion that coincides with the advent of consciousness.
Childhood experiences help to confirm or disprove the delusion.
USS 1 is so strong that we never really get over the delusion of
paramount importance and develop different ways to deal with the
contrary signals from the environment. Some people resentfully
accept that they are not as important as they feel, some are sporting
about the put-down messages from the world and some develop a
philosophical bent of mind and simultaneously understand that
every individual is wired to feel similar centrality which explains the
way people behave.

The upper newer layers of neurons are capable of evaluating new data and intellectual acceptance of facts happens here. Through the use of intelligent analysis, we learn to override the intrinsic delusion fuelled by USS 1 and corroborate or reject the insidious information received via mirror neurons, responding to the way other people treat us. Intelligent processes allow us to apply scientific knowledge to modulate emotions generated by subconscious centres through strength of reasoning. The process of acceptance can be considered complete when physiological upheaval generated by delusion or denial no longer occurs. The whole brain is thus involved in the task of putting ourselves in perspective.

Tan Tan: It certainly wouldn't do to have as many centres to the universe as there are people!

Me: Perception of relative size, scale and value of various elements of life is necessary for the maintenance of harmony—both in design and in social living. Various brain functions come together for the formation of balance in perceptions and such widespread integration demands connections, inter-connections and recursive channels of communication between brain regions to create such a relative perspective. One that is as close to reality and as objective as possible.

The ability to zoom out and view oneself with detachment in relation to the world does exist in the human brain as demonstrated by 'out of body experience' (OBE) on the electrical stimulation of the right angular gyrus (Blanke 2004). This (right angular gyrus) new brain area (neocortex) developed late in the evolutionary timeline. It communicates with a large spread of cortical areas, reading and balancing various inputs from multiple sense organs, and processes all of it to deliver perspective to the user. The primitive yet attractive illusion of self as the central player is thus transcended by the newly evolved competence to contemplate the self as a participant relative to other creatures and within a social structure.

From experiments that evoked 'OBE' by the stimulation of the angular gyrus it seems that the ability to distance and observe the self is an intrinsic higher brain function and can be evoked voluntarily. Humans can choose to 'become a witness' of the self and be objective about the person we are witnessing.

Tan Tan: That would be me? That could be funny!

Me: It gives us the opportunity to laugh at ourselves and not take self too seriously. Do be careful that you are using your own mind to observe and not someone else's opinion.

Tan Tan: Okay, here I go. I zoom out and am a fly on the ceiling and looking down on Tan Tan.

Me: Felix Baumgartner went up 39 kilometres and looked down at earth. He said when he got back, 'Sometimes you have to go up really high to see how small you really are'.

Tan Tan: I saw the photos taken from the Voyager 1 space probe. The earth was just a dot.

Me: And Carl Sagan reminded us about the wars, destruction and bloodshed inflicted upon this fragile planet by the very species that has been gifted with adequate intelligence to perceive such a perspective. We're well into the discussion on USS 10, that is, the 'Sense of Proportion'. Putting self in perspective with everything else and gaining a perspective about what matters, what is of topmost priority at this moment and how serious are the things, we are spending our energy and attention upon.

Tan Tan: My art teacher says, 'I need to learn to draw things in correct proportion'. She says, 'I need to be observant'. I didn't bother to do the homework, but now I see why and I will do it. When I understand how important I am as a dot in a dot, I can explain that to the odious pompous monitor.

Me: USS 10—Sense of Proportion—will also indicate what we need to focus on. Your attempt to put someone else in their place may or may not be successful, but deeply knowing your own competence and significance is a more useful and enduring exercise.

Tan Tan: It's true, I do spend a lot of time planning how I'm going to corner the bully and cut down the pompousness of the monitor.

PERSPECTIVE ABOUT SELF

Me: Humility is the attitude that emerges from USS 10. 'Humility point' is the point of dynamic balance achieved as the self weighs its own worth in relation to the rest of the world. The process has to become an application that continuously runs in the background lest the prevailing delusion of self-importance (fuelled by USS 1) overturns perspective. Self-assessment must be as close to reality as possible, neither too high nor low. Caution against underplaying of abilities has to be exercised because lowering of perceived competence levels leads to inability to put skills to work. Individuals become underconfident and aim at lower targets than they are capable of achieving. They allow opportunities to go past, too diffident to take up a challenge. Refusing to raise the bar, they deprive themselves of the joy of achievement and growth. Stagnating individuals are also prone to reach for easy pickings provided by opportunities for corrupt practices, and this weakens the fabric of society.

Tan Tan: It's not enough for me to learn about USS 10 alone; everyone needs to learn!

Me: Personal development is not for just a few; we need a critical mass of quality individuals to make a vibrant society. The more, the merrier.

Balancing ego to reach humility point is a continuous and dynamic process. Teetering on seesaw between feel-good of enlarging self-esteem and feel-bad of being put in place among competitors from external perspective (Sen 2006), adults have to be able to assess their own ego fit because others stop giving feedback for fear of repercussion. Sense of proportion applied to the continuous process of ego balance is one of the many ways to utilize this ability.

We can all benefit by learning to engage relevant parts of the brain to exercise objective perspective taking and apply it to art, work, behaviour and ego management frequently enough to make it a behavioural pattern (habit).

Tan Tan: Balance was USS 8. Can't you stick to a sequence?

Me: Everything is connected, remember? This is the brain we're talking about! Where else have you come across the word 'balance'?

Tan Tan: Okay, I saw the vegetable seller using a balance to weigh tomatoes.

Me: Ah, I saw the same instrument held out by blindfolded lady's statue outside the courthouse!

Tan Tan: I like joining dots!

Me: What does Lady Justice use the balance for?

Tan Tan: To make fair judgements.

Me: And that connects us to USS 11.

Tan Tan: You're not serious?

Me: Seriously, don't you have a *sense of what is fair and what is not*?

Tan Tan: You bet, I do!

Me: How early do you think we catch on to unequal distribution?

Tan Tan: Baby brother has been getting the lion's share of attention, and I caught on to that long ago!

Me: The ability to be surprised by unfairness has been detected and documented by researchers at Max Planck Institute, Department of Evolutionary Anthropology (Schmidt and Sommerville 2011) in 15-month-old human babies showing that this sense is available to humans quite early. They theorized that these are behavioural traits and may be instilled by the observation of parental behaviours, imbibed non-verbally in the form of values. This surmise is yet to be proved through credible research methodology. As I write, we cannot yet point out a location in the brain where the information about fair treatment is processed, but we know that this perception develops early in humans. In other primate experiments, aggressive reactions have been observed in Capuchin monkeys, given inequitable rewards for equal work (Brosnan and de Waal 2003).

These experiments tell us that the equitable distribution of resources and cooperation are embedded in the evolutionary history of our species, and we are intrinsically wired with the ability to judge if a distribution is fair. Consequently, our brain and body react negatively, when we sense a violation of expected fair treatment. The violation of expectation and observation of discriminatory behaviour are perceived as threatening to well-being of the individual and society. USS 6—Threat Perception—sets off the HPA axis alarm that activates action stations and generates the full-blown physiological condition that we collectively call stress reaction.

Tan Tan: Oho! Now, you connected Lady Justice with stress.
Me: Look around, balance is required everywhere. As we get to the higher reaches of the brain, there are trillions of connections all over the place.
Tan Tan: You are all over the place too, jumping from USS 1 to 8 and 11 and 6. How am I to even start my Ninja training if you go on like this?

THE BRAIN CAN BE TRAINED

Me: An untrained brain is also all over the place. It does so many things at once, and it becomes good at doing some tasks, so they become easy, and then they become habits and some habits take over the brain.
Tan Tan: If I do something many times over and it becomes easy for me, then that is a skill, not a habit!
Me: They are different names for the same process, technical name being neuroplasticity.

Tan Tan: Habits are mostly bad!

Me: The bad ones can do hostile takeovers. Neuroplasticity has good and bad effects. Norman Doidge calls it the 'Plastic Paradox'. Now that we know how it works, we also know that you need not be stuck in a habitual groove. You can reclaim your brain.

Tan Tan: Too much of a good thing can be bad?

Me: Like overthinking. Humans can think and imagine scenarios that are yet to happen. This is a valuable and empowering competence. Feeling powerful is addictive, so we do more and more of it, until we can't seem to stop.

Tan Tan: Thoughts are not things?

Me: They are products of electrical activity buzzing between sets of neurons. Call it mental activity.

Tan Tan: Too much buzzing! What is buzzing, thoughts or my mind?

Me: Mind is the playground where we indulge by allowing thoughts to play around, a sort of stage built on an infrastructure of inter-connected nerve cells, and it can be as large and extensive as the architecture of the brain and the efficiency of function allows. Being a living organ system, it has blood supply, existing pathways and a chemistry that drives it.

Tan Tan: Existing paths like? Wait! Don't tell me—when my brother was born he already knew how to cry.

Me: Reflex paths are built in to ensure survival. They have come to be through evolution, a process of natural selection (passing on of successful traits via genetic succession). Humans are not just designed to survive, but built to thrive. Human brains are wired for social living and interdependence. We receive innate rewards in the form of a shot of dopamine when we connect with others and feel depleted when in isolation. The benefits of reward response trickle down to the immune cells and result in robustness and well-being.

Tan Tan: So, it's good for you that I hang around while you write, or you may have gotten sick if left all alone.

Me: [*Rolling my eyes*] Why does this conversation remind me of
USS 6, when we understood that pain is experienced identically
whether in physical or social context!

Tan Tan: Huh?

Me: I guess, you do help to keep a sort of balance.

Tan Tan: USS 8? [*Tan Tan holds his arms out and begin to walk on a
line between floor tiles.*]

Me: The sense of balance would also apply to physical as well as
social realms; though I can't quote a lab experiment to prove it,
we do need to conduct life with plenty of balance. Here we are
talking about the abstract concept of balance, which is finding
equilibrium between extreme positions. This is not USS 8.

Tan Tan: Can you give it another name?

Me: Let's call it 'poise'.

Tan Tan: Yeah, like am I the centre of the Universe or just a dot
in a dot? I am gracefully poised somewhere on that scene.

Me: We could coin a new word 'poise finder' that answers
questions like 'How much is too much' and identify the fine
line between challenge and stress.

One of the onerous tasks of leadership is to maintain poise. One way to begin the practice of poise is to become aware of the extreme ends of the spectrum and decide where you want to position yourself on that band. It is simplistic to aim for middle ground in every case. Intelligent processes are used to understand the concept of extremes, and the deeper gut feel of wisdom has to be tapped to decide on the chosen spot on the spectrum. Someone who has practised physical balancing poses, or walked a tight rope, knows that balance is a dynamic process and there can be no slackening while holding the pose. Leaders are under constant scrutiny and sometimes tire of maintaining poise in conduct and attitude. Developing fitness for sustained poise is both a physical and a mental requirement.

Tan Tan: The brain is anyway like a muscle.

Me: [*Reluctantly*] I'll agree with that for a while because the 'use it or lose it' principle applies to both.

Tan Tan: I'm in a bit of a hurry to be a Ninja leader, so tell me about the seesaw.

Me: Here is a table. The factors on two ends of the seesaw are not necessarily opposites or mutually exclusive but often pose a challenge for a leader to choose his spot.

	Chosen Position	
Enjoying life		Burning out
Task orientation		People orientation
Big picture perspective		Attention to detail
Competition		Ethics
Quality		Quantity/numbers
Growth		Exploitation
Self-interest		Altruism
Comfort		Novelty

Tan Tan: My brain is tired by just looking from left to right. Does every leader choose the same position on the spectrum?

Me: No, each chooses her/his own spot, and it all comes together as a unique style. That's why the middle column is blank, so you can decide where to hover.

Tan Tan: It could be pretty exhausting to be a leader! Does one get time out?

Me: As a leader in the making, you can practise 'poise' until it becomes second nature and a part of who you are. When a behaviour is put on in order to fulfil a leadership role, the pretending consumes a chunk of energy, leaving the individual with a depleted energy tank. That leader may fall off the tight rope.

Tan Tan: I start now?

Me: Never too early!

Tan Tan: I'm just a child! Have you seen children being poised?

Me: Yes, I have. And I have seen adults being extreme. Perhaps it's not about age, but about wisdom not being given a chance to express itself. That comes from using USS 7, by developing the skill of listening to the body and its level of enthusiasm.

Tan Tan: Does a child have wisdom?

Me: Shall we allow the reader to answer that?

HIGHER BRAIN LEVEL USSs

There are two higher brain level USSs. They are as follows:

USS 12

OPTIMISM

USS 13

PURPOSE

CHAPTER 10

IS IT USEFUL FOR
A NINJA TO FEEL LUCKY?

The Usss we are discussing and enumerating are rather insidious and intrinsic. They are like background running programmes that do not ask for applause or acknowledgement, so we take them for granted. Being overlooked and undervalued, they may wilt and wither from neglect and disuse, or get disabled due to repression, as observed in the case of empathy in health workers. On the other hand, lying below the radar of awareness, they could become overused and dominant, as in the case of sense of 'ego threat' which is a function of USS 6—Pain and Threat Perception—making individuals competitive, defensive or arrogant. The permutations and combinations of less or more expression of these background apps result in the formation of personality and attitude.

USS12: OPTIMISM

Tan Tan: The elder says, 'He doesn't like my "attitude"'. I have no idea what he wants me to change, so how am I going to even try? Yesterday he caught me trying to throw away the milk I was served at breakfast. [*Grimacing*] I hate the smell of milk—yuk!

Me: How much did you drink up?

Tan Tan: Half. The elder called me out, raised the glass for all the students to see and asked, 'Is this glass half full or half empty?'

Me: Then?

Tan Tan: He began a discourse right there in the mess hall. I wasn't listening, just thanking my stars that I didn't have to drink it.

Me: You got caught and still escaped torture and punishment!

Tan Tan: Hee hee, I'm a lucky person!

Me: That's a positive bias; USS 12 is also known as 'Optimism'. If you had listened to the discourse, it could have been on the same subject. The ability to bet on a favourable outcome in an uncertain world is based on the function of the left inferior frontal gyrus. It is able to override motor responses, thereby inhibiting actions based on basic functions such as fear and anxiety. When we have some good predictions and some bad, we may press on regardless of the possibility of failure, which puts us in a position that is more likely to succeed than the people who did not even try.

Tan Tan: Phew! Is it useful for a Ninja to feel lucky?

Me: Turns out that feeling lucky as an attitude rather than as a superstition is useful for every professional, especially entrepreneurs and financiers. For every leader, feeling lucky unlocks a rush of feel-good, though the conditions and reality are still the same. The bad news creates an internal environment that focuses attention on a narrow band of negative possibility causing anxiety that maintains the narrow range of attention. Optimism, on the other hand, puts the negativity aside and opens up the spot beam of attention to a wider than usual angle, thereby allowing creative thought, energy for risk taking and enough bandwidth to create a safety net and escape routes in case things don't work out. The possibilities of failure are visible, but the brain prefers to look at the silver lining.

Tan Tan: Ray of hope! Where did I put my lucky charm!

Me: No no, 'Hope'—USS 3—is way down deep in the limbic mid-brain, hence is quite irrational and subconscious, but 'Optimism'—USS 12—is placed high up here (tapping the forehead just left of the midline) in the top and front of the brain, very conscious and new age. People with a strong optimism bias are upbeat and like to venture where no one has been before.

They are aware about the probability of failure, but don't allow the information to step on the brakes. They focus on the bright side and motivate themselves to strive to reach the bright spot. They release the chemicals associated with the anticipation of success, and these counter stress and anxiety during the struggle. This attitude enhances the chance of achieving and keeps the physiology healthier than the fearful and anxious states.

Tan Tan: [*Wide-eyed*] To boldly go where no man has ever gone before! Could be scary?

Me: They could be wrong. The unknown is really that—unknown. Unrealistic risk assessment and projections have created bubbles and they did burst with messy consequences, but risk takers are the ones who progress by leaps and bounds, succeeding and thriving on an evolutionary scale handing down the genes for optimism through generations.

> *Behold the turtle, he makes progress only when*
> *he sticks his neck out.*
>
> —James Bryant Conant

Unlike hope, which holds an imaginary picture of a specific outcome (expectation), optimism does not have a focused agenda or a plan. It manifests through preferential weightage given to good news with a relative denial of gloomy possibilities and is open to accepting the unexpected. The lucky charm belongs to the 'hope and belief' level of USS 3. Here at level 12, it goes by the name of 'risk appetite'.

Tan Tan: When I am picking Ninjas for my team, I will check for optimistic attitude. While making plans I will remind them about things that can go wrong, and while moving forward I will pump them up with all the wonderful surprises that are shining out from behind the clouds.

Me: Optimism is learnable (Seligman 1998). We can examine our own levels of optimism/pessimism and build on the positive bias. In the beginning, like all learning, it will take some effort and intention. A disaster is a good place to begin. We appreciate the blackness of where we find ourselves, and then list out the good that may come from the situation. Say, when your team loses a game very badly.

Tan Tan: That's a familiar situation. What good may come out of that! Ha, yes pompous monitor would be less pompous for a while!

Me: A coach could sit down with you and make you see where you are going wrong and practise the particular moves your players are terrible at. You become a better team.

Tan Tan: So, I begin with shipwreck scenes and purposely make myself see the silver lining, and each time I do the exercise, I get better at it. Disasters come in plenty.

Me: And then you can teach yourself to see the bright side when both probabilities, good and bad, are put in front of you. The optimistic bias has a tendency to look at the bright side, yet because this USS resides in the cognitive brain, we can caution ourselves not to be 'blind optimists' and ensure that the bright side does not dazzle so much that we miss the gloomy fine print altogether. That's necessary because when a task is undertaken for the very first time, no one knows what to expect.

Tan Tan: Still scary… Why would I even want to venture into the unknown?

Me: So that the 'unknown' will then become 'known'. When you make a new discovery how do you feel?

Tan Tan: I put my head into a hollow tree trunk, just to see what I could find in there. It could have been something that bites. But guess what? I found a squirrel's nest and it had three baby squirrels!

Me: Aww, and how did you feel?

Tan Tan: Very excited and energetic! I got all my friends to come and see. Felt important too!

Me: Tan Tan 'the discoverer'. That's pure joy! That is what drives exploration, research and invention. The need to *understand and know* is a higher level need, and effective motivator and getting to know something new gives us pure joy.

Tan Tan: I don't really like people who know a lot; they argue and fight, and feel happy when things go wrong with me. They wag their fingers and say, 'Told you so!'

Me: Tan Tan, people have needs and most have a need to feel comparatively better than others. We acknowledge that we can have needs; now try to acknowledge that in others. Just to remind you, here is the list again:

- Need to belong
- Need to connect
- Need for esteem
- Need to control/need for certainty
- Need to understand/know

At the level we're discussing now, another big need that has to be included is as follows:

- Need to contribute to the world

Tan Tan: What if the shiny thing behind the cloud is dangerous?

Me: Could be. This is the rational thinking zone, so foolhardiness won't do, but the unknown is unknown and could be a wondrous opportunity waiting to be discovered.

Tan Tan: But what if...

Me: What about 'what if'?

Tan Tan: If things go wrong, everyone will laugh at me, and the ones who warned me will say, 'Told you so!'

Me: So you're itching to try something out, but you're held back by the probability of failing? By what the others will say and the social pain of ridicule?

Tan Tan: They already have so much to say about the way I am!

Me: You will have to decide on what is more important to you. The opinion of your critics or the adventure. You are, of course, welcome to continue to live in the comfort of the palace of what is already known.

Tan Tan: That is boring! I really do want to know. I'll take the adventure and ignore the 'told you so' sayers.

Me: Wanting to know gives you power to put aside the possible discomfort of achieving nothing or getting bitten when you put your head in the hollow. You're willing to fail?

Tan Tan: Yes.

Me: Wow! The threat of 'social pain' (ego threat) that is inevitable with failure is circumvented by the push of 'curiosity'. That is why David Marcum and Steven Smith say in their book *Egonomics* that curiosity can balance out ego. Wanting to know the whole truth is the want-power that drives optimism. The urge to know is so strong that one is willing to set aside the probability of mortification of returning empty handed. In many people, the fear of failure is so big that they put roadblocks in their own path and hold back from making a bid for their own dream!

Tan Tan: I feel brave! I like 'want-power'. I heard about 'willpower' but not 'want-power'. What comes first?

Me: Want-power comes first. You must know what you want, then you will find the energy and the 'will' to go and get it. Even move the roadblocks planted by fears.

Tan Tan: Wanting is not greedy?

Me: Not, if there is a 'why' which upholds a core value. I want to know and understand to find out the whole truth. When I find out an undeniable truth, it becomes a legacy, a gift to all who care to know.

Tan Tan: My 'why' sometimes leads to 'because I want to look good compared to pompous monitor'.

Me: Not a universal core value, but it could be your current driver. When you introspect, you may not find respect for your current driver. Then you may 'want' to change what's in the core, because you know the 'why' of change is a worthy one.

Tan Tan: I must remember that wanting is not greedy if it upholds a worthy value. And a need is a body biology requirement, such as air, water and food.

Me: And safety, sex and social connection.

Tan Tan: You also listed social connection, need for control, to understand and to have purpose. How do these connect with body requirement? Sounds more like luxury, not essential.

USS 13: PURPOSE

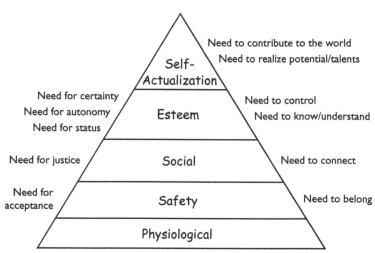

Figure 10.1 Maslow's Pyramid of Needs
Source: https://en.wikipedia.org/wiki/Maslow%27s_hierarchy_of_needs

Me: Let me tell you a story about a talented female theatre actor. Her name was Anamika. As a struggling artiste, she found it hard to make ends meet. She worked hard and gradually earned significant wealth. Along with her success, her social circle grew to include the rich and famous. From among her many suitors, she chose the richest, a man who owned large estates and industries, named Tilak Raj. Once married, she moved to the palatial heritage residence and enjoyed the glamour and luxury of her new life until she got terribly bored. She didn't have to work at memorizing scripts, rehearsing and performing, and wondered why she missed the dingy wings of the theatre and bustle of the greenroom. As she grew wistful and distant, her looks faded and health deteriorated. The best doctors were called in and numerous servants nursed her with care. Anamika asked her husband to allow her to return to the city and the theatre. Of course, he would have none of that, so she conspired with a handmaiden and ran away. Tilak Raj was powerful enough to track her down within a week. He found her living with the maid in rented rooms in a poorer part of town. What surprised him was that she looked strong and her eyes sparkled with what seemed to be a fire within. She said that she had to continue to make a difference to audiences through messages of social awareness that theatre brings to the world. Instinctively, he felt respect well up for her as a professional person and decided, against forcing her to return, to continue as his trophy wife. Before he left, he paid the landlord secretly in advance for six months being confident that Anamika would rebuild her life in that time.

Tan Tan: Perhaps Anamika was as bored as Prince Siddhartha in the palace and preferred the struggle to survive and find answers.

Me: Avoidance of suffering does not provide fulfilment.

Tan Tan: What ever does fulfilment feel like?

Me: Humans are endowed with a bulky neocortex equipped to solve problems. As long as this ability is challenged and engaged, one feels fulfilled. An individual constantly finds problems to solve and tasks to complete. The perception of redundancy and unused potential leads to discontent. The search for one's calling is incessantly scanning the environment. The discontent and disquiet are experienced, but due to the pressure of earning a livelihood and fulfilling lower level needs, there may not be an opportunity to investigate the cause for disquiet. This quest may never make it to the conscious level of thought, but the existing hunger initiates restlessness and motivates seemingly irrational action.

Tan Tan: Hunger? For using more of the brain?

Me: Yes, why waste such a wondrous gift? Hunger is a word we often swap with 'need'.

Tan Tan: It would be sad if I got a shiny new toy and didn't unpack it! The 'use it or lose it' principle would ruin it in no time! Why didn't Anamika know the difference between money and fulfilment? She was a grown-up person.

Me: Perhaps the urgent needs of lower levels of the pyramid were asserting themselves. Once those are taken care of ...

Tan Tan: Realization dawns!

Me: Realization of potential, meaning turning possibility into something 'real' is another name for 'self-actualization' that Abraham Maslow put at the summit of the *Pyramid of Human Needs* (Figure 10.1).

Deep sadness brought on by untapped potential leaves a biological scar mediated by neurotransmitters of frustration and restlessness. You will regret not using your best gifts endlessly, especially if you never found out what they were.

The immediacy of the chase for profit, wealth or career causes a person to ignore the gnawing emptiness caused by not being aligned with a worthy purpose, the urge to make a significant contribution to the world. She/he goes through life robbed of the passionate joy of a calling and functions at a plane of low energy and mediocrity.

When the question is asked of the self 'Are you enjoying life?' 'If not, then why not?' and 'If not now, then when?', the answers will lead us to the spirit of purpose which we will name USS 13.

Tan Tan: So is that a need or a sense, something I perceive?

Me: If needs are what an individual must take from the Universe, then purpose would translate into what the individual wants to give back to the world/Universe. Being aware of such a driving force is a perception of high order, and it is in line with deeply embedded values, so it spans all levels, involving emotion that makes enthusiasm available to take action in line with purpose.

Tan Tan: How can I find what my purpose is?

Me: We don't 'find' purpose, we CREATE it.

Tan Tan: Make up something random? No no, something in line with values!

Okay, what if I have a different purpose for each day?

Me: Purpose acts like an internal compass. Having a purpose saves our time and energy, so we are not spreading ourselves thin by running in all directions like a headless chicken may. It's fine to reset the purpose for each day as a conscious intention. It lends clarity to action. Clarity brings focus that couples which aligning with core (values) and releases a wellspring of zeal—a winning combination of ingredients for excellence.

Tan Tan: Knowing what I want to do and why, and having enough energy to do it, sounds useful, but I need to make my purpose something that I respect. Perhaps pulling pompous monitor out of his pompousness is not respectable enough. It'll have to be a Ninja-level purpose for Tan Tan. Let me think.

Me: Inspirational leaders help people uncover their inner compass and introduce meaningfulness into work. Motivation through this route is self-sustaining, as it unlocks energy that was awaiting a signal of Acknowledgement from the conscious brain. Interim achievements in the path to purpose are rewards in themselves because each step brings us closer to realizing the purpose. The chemical mechanism of endogenous recognition and rewards (dopamine) is empowering.

A private celebration within our own skin is such an awesome feeling that it renders external recognition redundant. A reward from outside at this juncture seems incidental and welcome, but not essential, because real celebration happens on the inside. Step-wise reward responses enhance brain function enabling 'flow' state, thereby releasing endogenous hormones of happiness (endorphin) as a side effect.

Joy experienced as a side effect of walking the path of purpose is a true joy and a renewable joy because we remain on that path and keep walking.

A 'Sense of Purpose' (USS 13)—also called the 'Spirit of Purpose'—is the perception of having filled the need for a 'why' for what you do. If there is a vacuum in place of the 'why' or even an unworthy reason for what we do, USS 13 generates a restlessness and pushes us to find the answer to the 'why' question. When a worthy purpose forms itself, it may be unspoken but present, and then USS 13 generates enthusiasm and helps to overcome hurdles and frustrations in the path that leads to achievement.

Me: A purposeless person is vulnerable to be seduced to internalize someone else's purpose.

Tan Tan: I am safe, I have the Ninja purpose. That's why I didn't join the bully's gang.

Me: You didn't tell me 'why' you want to train as a Ninja.

Tan Tan: Uh, I will have to think that one through.

Me: When you have a 'why', then ask 'why' of that why.

Tan Tan: Where will that take me?

Me: To your 'noble purpose'. A purpose that is so big that you may not achieve it in your lifetime, but because you blazed that trail, others will be inspired to carry your torch forward. It becomes your legacy.

Tan Tan: What's your noble purpose?

Me: Umm...

Tan Tan: Hee... hee... Gotcha! I've got a Ninja purpose and you don't ....

Me: 'To create a world of peace and beauty by unlocking intrinsic potential'.

Tan Tan: Uh? Come on! Can you be taking on the whole world?

Me: I told you the noble purpose need not be achievable in my lifetime, but I can work towards it through a mission. Since I have one, I don't feel bored or lonely.

Tan Tan: So, what's your mission? How do you unlock intrinsic potential?

Me: By helping people to minimize stress and proactively maximize the realization of potential through awareness about the neurology of emotions. I coach people to remove roadblocks they put in their own way.

Tan Tan: You know, I think you're using the pretty word 'purpose' when you could easily say 'goal'.

Me: Not really, a sense of purpose is the motivation to make a bid for the goal. USS 13 is inside a person, and a goal is out there in the world. Purpose is also described very simply as *Ikigai* in Japanese. It translates to 'Why I wake up in the morning'. Figure 10.2 is a diagrammatic form of *Ikigai*.

Tan Tan: That which you can be paid for, I'd like to get paid. When did Mr Maslow draw that pyramid of needs?

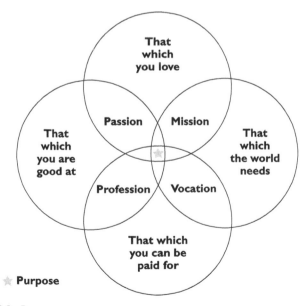

Figure 10.2. Purpose
Source: https://rolemodels.me/we-all-need-an-ikigai/

Me: He first proposed this theory in 1943.

Tan Tan: If I wrote that theory, I would just draw a pile of money at the bottom of the pyramid.

Me: But money can't buy belonging or respect.

Tan Tan: And we could get real bored being rich like Prince Siddhartha and Anamika?

Me: Maybe they asked themselves, 'Why am I here?'

Tan Tan: If we keep asking the 'why' question, then I guess everyone has a different 'why'. That's because my 'why' has to be in line with my value print, and that is mine and mine alone. Anamika was mixed up about what's important. You're also mixed up putting needs in a book on perceptions.

Me: When you're hungry, is that a perception?

Tan Tan: Umm yes... I kinda know, I need a snack. Okay okay... I get it. I have all the equipment to 'sense' the need.

Me: I need to belong, and when I fill up the requirement, I have a 'sense of belonging', and I go about my day with a 'sense of purpose' when I know 'why' I do and what I do. Without the fulfilment of higher order needs (understanding, control and purpose), we may survive, but do not thrive. Meaningless, helpless and ignorant existence does not even qualify as living. The prospect of these needs being fulfilled is potently motivating. Need-deprived persons do not discriminate about quality. They grab what they get.

Tan Tan: Understanding! I really need to understand things! Sometimes people refuse to explain.

Me: The human brain craves explanation. When knowledge is deficient, the imagination fills the gap with a story. It's interesting to compare mythology from different parts of the world. People far removed from each other have developed markedly similar explanations for the powers of the Universe, of what happens after we die and why diseases strike or how to heal from the damage they cause.

Tan Tan: My lucky charm protects me from getting sick.

Me: Does it really?

Tan Tan: Oh well, I guess not. It's not nice of you to break the spell.

Me: People do get annoyed when someone messes with their favourite story. The less that is known, the more preposterous the stories that can be woven around the question. The explanation is the closure the brain craves. Feed the brain an explanation, it accepts eagerly even if it is a half-baked, incredible and impossible to prove. A popular explanation may become deeply entrenched in the psyche of a population in the form of belief. If the whole community is indoctrinated with the same mythology, the strength of numbers lends credibility and conviction. Researchers who come up with scientific explanations later find stiff resistance when they disprove a popular belief. When Galileo disproved Ptolemy's geocentric theory about the Sun orbiting the Earth. The Holy Office of the Catholic Church even convicted Galileo as a heretic.

Tan Tan: But it's true! The Earth is just a dot.

Me: Science brings up undisputable facts. Occasionally scientific theories are disproved and data presented to shatter the old theory encounters resistance in scientific minds as well. But after due diligence science brings out the fact which is everybody's truth. On the other extreme lies fantasy which is nobody's truth.

Tan Tan: And what's in the middle?

Me: Somebody's truth. Part rational and part mythical. Often something based on what the person wants to believe.

Tan Tan: A Ninja can become invisible, right?

Me: Maybe science will make that happen someday. But belief and myth do endure and are handed down through centuries. Individuals and society both need the anchor provided by faith.

Tan Tan: Like religion?

Me: Equipped with intelligence that craves explanation, it becomes difficult to live in a world of uncertainty. We need faith to cope with an uncertain future and to answer existential questions.

Tan Tan: What if I'm not convinced by an explanation that is not backed by science? How then can I cope while science takes its time to search and research?

Me: You could believe in yourself?

Tan Tan: I can do that. I'm quite reliable.

Me: Trustworthy?

Tan Tan: You bet! Thank you, I feel good, strong and reliable. Pretty secure!

Me: You just used a sense of your own abilities and agency to lower the threat generated by uncertainty! Congratulations! Threat is sensed by USS 6, and USS 14 counters it.

Tan Tan: Fourteen! Does this USS have a name?

Me: Call it 'Sense of Power'.

USS 14
POWER AND CONTROL

USS 15
SENSE OF HUMOUR

CHAPTER 11

IS IT HARD TO CHANGE AN ATTITUDE?

The extent to which an individual perceives having personal agency and influence over outcomes, even if illusory, impacts emotional well-being, physiological state, immune function, cognitive performance, ability to cope with pain and stress, and the ability to make difficult behavioural changes. Studies show negative correlation between the perception of control and cardiovascular risk factors such as the amount of fat that collects around abdominal viscera (Cardarelli et al. 2011) and risk of diabetes mellitus (Cardarelli et al. 2007). The physiological consequences of this perception indicate its pivotal role. Control considerations have been studied more deeply in the form of 'learned helplessness' in animals. Lack of sense of control has been found to lead to depression (Chang and Sanna 2007), poor cognition, stress and hopelessness. Experiments conducted involved the measurement of cardiovascular risk factors in humans with correlation and cognitive tests taken under conditions of distraction in human subjects.

Tan Tan: You lost me there.
Me: When you have worked hard at studying a subject and are confident of being able to answer all the possible questions on the topic, how do you feel before the exam?
Tan Tan: Bring it on!
Me: When your basketball team has already won all the matches in the first round, how do you feel at the quarter finals?

Tan Tan: We feel sure that we'll win again. Our war cry is 'Yes we Can!'

Me: USS 14, 'Power and Control', is also known as self-efficacy, and a perception of having the competence to shape one's own life, perhaps influence others too. Elderly persons living in assisted conditions maintain better health if they feel their decisions and choices matter. I mentioned that the benefit from the perception is available even if the feeling is not really true (illusory).

'Sense of Power and Control' includes an assessment of:

- Competence
- Stamina
- Influence
- Agency
- Potential

Tan Tan: What if I believe that I am stronger than I really am?

Me: You may take on a bigger adversary than you are capable of fighting.

Tan Tan: I could get killed!

Me: What if you always picked a challenge that was lower than your capability?

Tan Tan: Then I wouldn't really know what I'm capable of!

Me: You would play small. That may please others, but it won't please you. Being accurate in assessing one's powers is a key to survival and to experience joy from meeting a challenge that is worthy of the individual's potential. USS 14 can be developed through experience.

Tan Tan: By winning or by losing?

Me: A little of both. How afraid are you of losing?

Tan Tan: Terrified! You're telling me, it's okay to lose? Other coaches push me to win!

Me: If you are willing to learn from it, you can benefit from losing. You're the one who impressed me by saying that you would choose to venture and fail rather than not try at all! Losing is the same as failing, isn't it?

Tan Tan: What's to learn from failing and or losing?

Me: The boundaries of your abilities. You can practise later and get better and better and enlarge those boundaries. If you're winning all the time, you will get complacent. Losing is good; it will cause you pain and push you to take action to win the next time. We have to be sporting enough to fail.

Tan Tan: Gna... gna... gna...

Me: Failing feels bad because we expect to win. Feelings are temporary. You can wait for the molecules causing an emotion to be mopped up. Then we can celebrate the learning we acquired from the loss and recover, regroup and work on improving the skill.

Tan Tan: Losing could get me killed during Ninja training.

Me: The ability to mentally assess the power of another individual in comparison with self is useful in pack animals. Societies require a leader. The position of a leader comes with status and privileges such as the display of respectful behaviour from others, first choice of mate and best portions of food. Individuals who assess themselves as worthy of being the leader vie with each other for the top spot. They challenge and fight each other. The one whose assessment was erroneous runs the risk of being killed. The genes of accurate assessors get carried to the next generation. Accurate assessors of power have the wisdom to refrain from challenging the overtly powerful candidate or must have the calibre and motivation to challenge and defeat all other contenders.

Tan Tan: USS 14 helps me to compare and rate myself and others! I'm not sure that is a good thing.

Me: It is an important skill, a survival tool, and ensures you choose tasks in line with your abilities. The trouble starts when we overuse it and establish a judgemental habit or attitude (Figure 11.1).

Figure 11.1. Judgemental Habit
Source: Author

Tan Tan: I don't like being compared with my cousins.

Me: Perhaps you do it silently anyway.

Tan Tan: Yeah, I do. Then I feel short, ugly, stupid and awkward.

Me: What do you think of the oldest cousin?

Tan Tan: He is the studious kind, and his sister is sporty. Not my type.

Me: You have little boxes with labels for everyone? Which is your box?

Tan Tan: I don't want to be in a box!

Me: When we overuse USS 14, we have stereotype slots into which we fit people, and it only follows that one of the boxes is 'your type'—that which you have to climb into.

Tan Tan: Uff, that's stuffy!

Me: Perhaps everyone feels stuffy in their little boxes?

Tan Tan: That way even I have to always behave a certain way—that's not freedom!

Me: You were calling people names like 'studious' and 'sporty'; perhaps you're doing some of that to yourself too?

Tan Tan: Mmm, yes; I call myself a skunk. Have done some bad things! I actually hate myself!

Me: That would be your inner critical system overacting and berating you with some moralistic judgements.

Tan Tan: Is it a part of USS 14?

Me: It's a parasite feeding off USS 14. Used to serve as a guide once; now it is a tormentor. When the inner critical system is used repeatedly, it grows strong and robust. It grows so big that you may mistake its conclusions and judgements as your own.

Tan tan: Oww, perhaps I have one already!

Me: You can recognize it from its patterns; in fact, it is merely a pattern of thoughts that has become a habit. If you can distinguish this self-running background programme, you can give it a name.

Tan Tan: Odious Big Bully.

Me: I usually call it the critical pig.

Tan Tan: No, pigs are nice. This one is a bully.

Me: OBB for short?

Tan Tan: Okay, what's the point of naming it? I just want it to get out of my head.

Me: Name it to tame it. You allowed it to grow by using it all the time, comparing with others to make yourself feel better about yourself. It worked, so you used it again and again. Now it is overpowering. To lose it, you just stop using it—just like getting over an addiction. Easier said than done, and you have to *want* to get over it.

Tan Tan: How do I stop it? I didn't even know it was beating me down from inside until you made me recognize it. It's all your fault.

Me: Hey!

Tan Tan: [*Running around the room in circles*] Now I have a bully outside and a bully in my head.

Me: Relax, OBB is just a friend who was allowed to become overbearing. Now you have to politely ask it to be quiet while you repair the leak of self-esteem it has caused you. I think you're grown up enough to refill your self-esteem tank on your own. OBB is a useful ally in emergency. You want it to shrink back to useful size and only use it as a quick reference guide.

Tan Tan: USS 14—Power and Control—will tell me what I'm capable of. If I don't allow my inner bully to put me down, then I can get an accurate idea about my abilities.

Me: Be careful, you don't overestimate your abilities! You know that could make you bite off more than you can chew.

Tan Tan: Another balancing act?

Kaushal is a responsible and hard-working young man. His older brother Kishore was apparently very successful. At the age of 28, his brother was politically well connected and had plenty of money, cars and enviable social standing. However, the family did not know what exactly Kishore did to achieve that status. Yet they often held up the example of Kishore to push Kaushal to be as successful, whereas Kaushal wanted to be a journalist and knew that it would be tedious and it was slow road to success. Suddenly, Kishore's fortunes crashed and he was penniless. Hiding from creditors, he had to depend on his farmer father for sustenance along with wife and children. Kaushal was younger, disapproved strongly of the older brother's ways, disapproved of his parents for encouraging his sibling who brought shame and financial strain on the family. They had already arranged their daughter's marriage to a family that expected a lavish wedding, and therefore had to resort to taking loans to fund such an event. Kaushal disapproved of a lot of things going on in the family but quietly resolved not to be like any of them, and continue to work honestly and live within his means. But immediately he was required to rescue the situation. Kaushal single-handedly shouldered the responsibility of conducting their sister's wedding, returned all loans and continued to send money home for daily expenses. Kaushal is now 32 and has finally fallen in love. Unfortunately, his girlfriend rejected his proposal and is refusing to speak with him or connect in any way. Kaushal spiralled into a breakdown triggered by the heartbreak. Today he is feverish, unwilling to eat or drink and unable to go to work. Kaushal's close friends got together and convinced him to seek my help. On examination, I find that Kaushal has been putting up a brave front to the world, including his closest friends. No one knows that he is soft and hurting inside since his last breakup eight years ago.

He is strongly critical about most people and can easily supply friends with sage advice and counsel, but today his breakdown has exposed his trembling and weakened inner being. His friends believe that he has an infection. After running medical tests and listening to his story, I could only detect a large parasitic *inner critic* that helps Kaushal point out the mistakes of others, but since the parasitic *critic* is so large, it turns its full critical gaze inwards onto Kaushal himself. Not being able to counter so much self-criticism, Kaushal is exhausted, low on self-worth. Rejection of his sincere proposal was the final straw that broke the back of his fragile self-esteem. Together we worked on helping Kaushal to recognize and tune down the critical patterns of thought. This helped him to climb out of the pit of despair. The recovery was slow but enduring. He is now aware of and able to interrupt the instinctive and habitual pattern of mental comparison as soon as he finds himself indulging. Interrupting and aborting the critical system have weakened the circuit. Kaushal now knows that the *inner critic* is merely a habit of thought and had the power to lower his opinion of self. Having identified and isolated the pattern, he is in a position to use it when required and ignore or turn it off at will.

Tan Tan: That was Kaushal meeting his own OBB.

Me: This (USS 14) is the perception I wrote about in my first book *Get the Ego Advantage!*. Did you read it?

Tan Tan: Naah, I'm too young to read self-help books! But I saw the Superman cartoon!

Me: I used the metaphor of the Lycra suit that just fits, not too tight, not too loose—that contains the package of abilities and social worth. The suit denotes the boundaries of that perception and I called it 'ego'.

Tan Tan: And 'ego threat' is anything that threatens that boundary? Like OBB? And punches holes in the self-esteem tank?

Me: Yes; now we know that the perception of threat is located way down alongside USS 6, where the brain also perceives threat to the physical body. But the sense of 'Power and Control', USS 14, is a function of the higher cognitive brain, a far more evolved function that has proactive role in bidding for leadership positions. Competing, comparing and judging are adjuvant functions. Any of these could flip into overdrive and throw us off ego balance.

The struggle to build a sense of 'Power and Control' (USS14) in the face of ego threat (USS6) leads to a shaky insecure perception of power, and we try to stand firm by enlarging the function of comparing and being judgemental, finding excuses to berate and downgrade others and consequently feel secure. This is not sustainable without continuing the cycle of comparison and fault-finding incessantly. When we find ourselves being overjudgemental, we need to interrupt the tendency and replace it with curiosity and find positive things to feel about the self without comparing. An overactive habit of comparison turns the judgemental machinery on to the self.

Tan Tan: The judge is in overdrive and has inflated itself into my tormentor OBB. He has a name now, but I don't know how to make him shut up.

Me: Get curious. Try to find out more about the things you don't know. The judge inside our head is a product of 'I know what is right and wrong', and curiosity is the pin that punches a hole in the gasbag of Mr 'Know It All'. If we can remind ourselves that there is a lot we don't yet know, things we are confused about, how things look from another person's perspective, then we can squish the inner judge to a decent manageable size.

Come here and draw a cartoon of how you imagine the OBB looks like.

Tan Tan draws a figure with a large laughing head and unkind eyes. He draws drops of saliva making it slobber, and as an afterthought draws a judge's wig on the head. We laugh heartily, and Tan Tan's mood improves.

The perception of self-efficacy and agency could be extrapolated to include 'autonomy' or freedom to make our own decisions, something humans are willing to die for. Competent professionals are known to choose autonomy over higher pay and perks, leading Daniel Pink to name autonomy as the first one of the three factors that fundamentally motivates humans (Pink 2011).

USS 15: SENSE OF HUMOUR

Tan Tan: Don't tell me being funny is a USS!

Me: Humour is taken very seriously by neuroscientists. The stress-reversing role of mirthful laughter was studied and reported in 1989 (Berk et al. 1989).

'He who laughs, lasts' is a quote ascribed to Alfred E. Neuman (the fictitious mascot for *MAD* magazine) and it seems to suggest that a person who is endowed with a sense of humour is able to cope with stress and pull through hard times.

Tan Tan: I look for friends who have a sense of humour.
Me: I would like a life partner who likes a good laugh.

Study of deficits in humour appreciation and comprehension have been undertaken by neuroscientists in persons with focal brain damage, identifying the right frontal lobe as essential in this very human function of amusement (Shammi and Stuss 1999). The ability to hold information long enough to appreciate the twist in a tale is called 'working memory' and is necessary for both verbal and non-verbal humour appreciation. Factors such as verbal abstraction, mental shifting, ability to focus attention and to search the environment for incongruity, all participate in the generation of merriment. A robust sense of humour is thus indicative of a healthy brain substrate that otherwise participates in other serious cognitive processes, episodic memory and self-awareness.

Tan Tan: Being funny is a lot of brain work!
Me: Humour is intelligence in disguise! Brainy people are not always socially smart. But brainy people with all-round brain development can guess how other people think and react. The ability to read intentions of others is of vital protective significance in social animals. We need to know whom to trust to be socially effective. Neuroimaging studies on humour processing uncover the involvement of the left hemisphere including the cerebellum; these are shared areas that are also activated during tasks of attribution of intention (Bartolo et al. 2006). If we develop the brain for the interpretation of intention of others, we simultaneously develop a capacity for humour.
Tan Tan: I can read intention means that I know you are coming to greet me and hug me or perhaps you mean to hurt me and snatch my sandwich.

Me: Some people can't tell, and that's a big social handicap.

Tan Tan: Circus clowns do make me laugh, but I don't really see them as smart.

Me: Slapstick humour is based on the element of surprise, the timing and incongruity. We laugh and the experience becomes an enjoyable and memorable one. The left amygdala (emotional centre) is activated in the subjective experience of amusement. The emotional dimension helps to make a fun-filled experience memorable by facilitating the memory centre (hippocampus).

Involvement of both hemispheres of the brain—the limbic cortex and cerebellum—makes humour a whole-brain activity. A person displaying capacity for humour can be assumed to be well endowed with connections between various brain regions; such inter-connections drive cognitive intelligence, social intelligence, positive affect, focus, morale and perseverance.

Funny people (like the court jester) may throw up absurd and incongruous solutions, but the laughter they invoke lightens the atmosphere making it conducive to creative thinking, stimulating others to think out of the box and contribute some seriously bright ideas.

Tan Tan: Can I learn to be funny?

Me: Like many other neurological functions, humour is trainable. Awareness about the importance of humour in daily life, at the workplace, in leadership, teamwork, stress relief and in developing resilience is the first step. Once the importance is clear, there is inner motivation to seek out exercises and activities that will nurture this talent.

Tan Tan: If humour is a talent, why are you calling it a 'sense'?

Me: Developing this competence makes you perceptive of absurdity and incongruity of a situation and how it connects laterally through similar sounding words or seemingly unrelated events. Perceiving humour in a situation immediately sidesteps the stress and anxiety of a difficult circumstance, lightens interpersonal tension and defuses conflict. A tense situation narrows focus towards a problem, but as the brain perceives the funny side, focus opens its spot beam to a wide beam and helps the brain to come up with creative solutions.

Tan Tan: You may perceive the humour and not share it.

Me: Maybe later with an appropriate audience.

Tan Tan: Could be difficult.

Me: First, you have to practise not to laugh at your own joke and to keep a straight face even when you're giggling inside.

Tan Tan: What if the others don't realize that I was being funny?

Me: It means you read the audience wrongly. You need more training. Not laughing when you are tickled is an exercise in impulse control. Since humour is whole-brained a lot of skills contribute to the training. Even music practise can be humour training.

Tan Tan: Now you're joking!

Me: In music lessons, you can learn voice modulation, rhythm and pausing for effect. Music can teach us many things, especially emotional expression, perseverance and harmony.

Tan Tan: I'm terrible at singing.

Me: That makes you a better candidate for training. You have to learn to laugh at yourself, your terrible crooning and not take yourself seriously. The process of training develops tracts of the brain that were lying unused. We may train at something we're terrible at and grow only marginally better at the activity, but the neurons and circuits that are strengthened in the process contribute to the overall growth of brain capacity. This could manifest in unexpected ways. When you judge yourself as a 'terrible' singer, you are exercising the OBB. When you drew a cartoon of OBB, you used your sense of humour and made him look funny.

Tan Tan: OBB is in my head, and I poked fun at a part of me. That made me feel better about myself! Is that strange?

Me: When we can make jokes at our own expense, we put others at ease by displaying our own comfort and openness. Humour is disarming, defuses tensions and builds bonds. When the joke is on you, there is no risk of someone else being offended. To make up jokes about yourself, you have to zoom out and look at yourself from a distance using the app located in the angular gyrus around the top of your ear that we named USS 10 (Sense of Proportion). That is a spiritual exercise (be a witness) and will result in humility and help in creating perspective. Detecting humour in a situation can pull you up from a position of low self-esteem to a healthy range. The same sense can lessen the pain that inevitably accompanies being put (put down) in one's place from receiving criticism. Retaining humility within, one can still exaggerate and caricature for the sake of obtaining humorous effect.

Being comical demands genuineness and the courage to bring one's weaknesses out in the open. Daring to be vulnerable and to be able to joke about it opens the floodgates of trust. Dr Brené Brown in his book *Daring Greatly: How the Courage to Be Vulnerable Transforms the Way We Live, Love, Parent, and Lead* explains how the display of trust wins hearts of people who then respond by returning that gift of openness (Brown 2012).

WILL IT BE HARD TO CHANGE ONE'S ATTITUDE?

Placed within uncomfortable and adverse conditions, the human organism (just like any other living thing) instinctively moves to a place of relative comfort, taking refuge from the harshness of the surroundings. This instinct is central to survival; yet the same basic tendency manifests in complex creatures as avoidance, and even denial, and gets in the way of wholehearted courageous living. Ensconced within a zone of familiarity and relative comfort, the top-heavy evolved neocortex experiences redundancy. Not being used, it tends to wither.

A warning to humans who resist moving out of their comfort zone is the life story of a quaint sea creature, the sea squirt (tunicate) which is a tadpole-like chordate animal with the spinal cord and primitive brain, an eye and a tail to help it swim. As soon as the creature finds a place that is comfortable and offers it all the resources it needs to survive, it attaches itself to the spot. There it lives for the rest of its life. Now that it no longer needs to hunt or move, it finds no use of the brain and quickly auto-digests that useless organ. Now it will only need to detect the conditions of the environment, but the cell wall of surface tissues is capable enough to fulfil that function.

Tan Tan: Every cell can do some sensing? You mean every cell can do brain work?

Me: The work of the brain is to help the organism to interact with and navigate the environment. We tend to think of the nucleus of the cell as being its brain, but we find the brain-like functions are executed by the cell wall—the interface between the organism and the environment. In complex organisms, the same work is done by the special senses, and the social dynamics are taken care of by USSs that we have detailed in this book.

Tan Tan: But the cell wall is just a transparent membrane! I drew that diagram in class.

Me: Just to keep things in perspective, let us remind ourselves that the nervous system grows from the ectoderm of the embryo. Ecto means the outer layer—the boundary with the environment. We were talking about choosing between comfort and harsh conditions, and it goes without question that living things opt for comfort once the senses (nerve systems) detect the quality of the surroundings.

Tan Tan: Yes, avoid the harsh surroundings and stay where the comforts are. Sniff... sniff..., I smell muffins.

Me: I baked a batch, but they're not for you.

Tan Tan: What do you mean? Of course, I get to eat at least one?

Me: How did you presume that?

Tan Tan: Because I am cute!

Me: That's a terribly lame argument and an entitled attitude.

Tan Tan: I've not been called that word before. Is 'entitled' good or bad?

Me: Entitlement is a very big problem with humans today. It's a modern epidemic of belief. It strikes young humans who are used to having their own way and having it immediately, on demand. That is why they have pathetically untrained circuits for restraint. They refuse to wait for what they want and the belief runs so deep that a lot is taken for granted. They will protest when a comfort is denied but scarcely notice when it is provided.

Tan Tan: There is also this word you grown-ups use to talk down to kids. I still don't know what 'attitude' means.

Me: Attitude is a standpoint. You approach all situations from that point which was created by belief about your position. A sort of imaginary pedestal. Cuteness worked in your favour before and now you're presumptuous about the power it gives you. Family wealth or influence, good looks and previous sexual conquests could add to the height of the pedestal. The entitled attitudes I see in young adults make me so sad.

Tan Tan: Why does that make you sad?

Me: If you believe your cuteness got you the muffin, you will not feel grateful.

Tan Tan: But I will feel smug.

Me: The ungrateful will be deprived of joy. The taken for granted comfort is just a part of the furniture, so there is nothing to be joyous about.

Tan Tan: Oh!

Me: Have you ever noticed or been grateful for the air you breathe?

Tan Tan: That's crazy! How will I say thank you with every breath? I will be squashed under a mountain of gratefulness for air, water, sun, everything!

Me: No Tan Tan, gratefulness doesn't mean writing 'Thank You' cards or carrying a burden of obligation. Gratefulness is just acknowledging in your heart and appreciating the presence of something that is useful to you, even attention and effort made by someone else for you. That Acknowledgement changes the way activation patterns occur in your brain (Zahn et al. 2009), as well as increases blood flow to the left frontal lobe which changes mood to the positive state and irrigates the hypothalamus which controls a host of hormones via the pituitary gland. These dynamics completely reverse the pattern mandated by stress, lowering cortisol (stress) and increasing dopamine (reward). This grateful blood flow pattern is a pattern of abundance. It nourishes the most advanced parts of the brain that participate in creative thought and analysis. It makes the conditions suitable for the experience of joy. It is a very personal internal flip switch.

Tan Tan: Can gratefulness become an attitude, a standpoint?

Me: Why not? Do it once, the feeling of reward tells you to do it again, and then you become good at invoking gratefulness even at will. It can be a place you're coming from, and a way of life.

Tan Tan: Will it be hard to do? To change one's attitude?

Me: Resistance to change is a very basic law of physics called the 'law of inertia'.

Tan Tan: I know that one! It's Newton's first law. But in the brain?

Me: A quantum of energy is required to propel a person from out of a familiar zone and to make a change. Resistance to change is a veil that prevents a clear view of reality. Inertia will keep thwarting your half-hearted efforts to enlarge the boundaries of familiarity. Fears will raise their dragon heads and blow more smoke into the haze. As you can see, neither 'entitlement' nor 'inertia' will allow you to grow or even get a clear view of reality. The brain is the organ that is supposed to put us in touch with the real environment, but here we are languishing in a static state of comfort and allowing the brain to atrophy from disuse. In this fugue state behind a smokescreen that blocks us from reality, we develop imaginary explanations for the little we do see. These unsubstantiated explanations are named 'ideology' because they are based on theoretical ideas not backed by facts. The lazy brain instinctively warms up to ideas and explanations that confirm its presumptions. This phenomenon is called 'confirmation bias'. It keeps us removed from reality.

Tan Tan: I rather like my standpoint. Why do I have to go and meet reality? I hear it bites!

Me: There is no other place to live other than the real world. Reality does not alter with belief, comfort or delusions of entitlement. Reality, sooner or later, does bite the unprepared. You can do yourself a favour by being equipped to handle it. Confront reality and embrace it entirely.

Tan Tan: Like go and hug that cactus!

Me: You want to stay in the make-believe world inside the palace?

Tan Tan: As a Ninja, I have to fight the bad guys and their evil designs. Training myself inside the artificial life inside the 'palace' won't do.

Me: You will not know what you're up against, and you may find out late that your training within the Ivory tower is obsolete. A leader has to have futuristic vision, and you have to be 'out there' to get wise. Get trained in handling stress and processing it chemically in your body, so your system is capable and strong. Coping with stress comes from doing, not from watching videos or reading a self-help book.

Tan Tan: Endurance training is tough. The physical coach keeps yelling 'discipline'. Keeping discipline is his job, but he keeps yelling at us.

Me: To confront reality in all its brutality, one requires discipline. The brain is good at going into denial and sweeping unprocessed emotions under the carpet into the subconscious cellar. Discipline is really an inside job. A function of the regulatory pathways like the one you used to delay eating the cookie till the end of a chapter. It is self-regulation. The main path runs through a strap of nerve tissue named OFC. Exercising this tissue to robust efficient levels helps in connecting emotional and cognitive levels, thereby allowing the incorporation of emotional information in decision-making, calming the emotional centre, putting aside discomfort long enough to allow the thinking brain to come up with the most appropriate response and adapting to novel situations. Discipline includes a range of functions. Some of them are as follows:

• Regulation of emotion to respond rather than react
• Adaptability
• Ability to delay gratification
• Taking responsibility for one's own part
• Being balanced in judgement

Tan Tan: Ninja training is for laser sharp focus, but my attention keeps jumping around. I wish, wish and wish to be a great Ninja!

May your wishes all come true
May you always do for others
And let others do for you
(Lyrics of *Forever Young* by Bob Dylan)

Tan Tan: Do wishes come true in the real world?
Me: That is the only true world Tan Tan. First you prepare for the real world by learning to be independent, then you learn to balance your ego and learn to ask for help.
Tan Tan: I won't need help once I'm independent!
Me: You will be surprised. We humans live an interdependent life. We collaborate. Our brain is built for connection and collaboration. It is an egotistic delusion that makes us believe that we can thrive without the help of others. We're social animals.
Tan Tan: I don't want others to know that I can't manage me by myself.

Me: It is common knowledge. A mason built this room for me and a carpenter made this table. I didn't and couldn't create this computer by myself. We find interdependence difficult as long as we feel insecure because we are ashamed of being inadequate. We build walls and fortresses when insecure, but once we feel safe, we reach out to collaborate. Feeling secure and contented sets off a self-sustaining synergistic cycle. See Figure 11.2.

Tan Tan: Didn't you pay for the table?

Me: Yes, I did. That is why it is called 'interdependence'. You will see it as mutually beneficial only after you have accepted the abundance of the Universe and opened out your mind from the narrow focus of self-preservation to be able to appreciate the skill of the carpenter.

Tan Tan: [*Breathing long and deep*] Abundance feels quite comfortable. I almost miss the buzzing in my head.

Me: Buzzing?

Tan Tan: Thoughts! Lot's of thoughts. [*Wuzzz buzz*]

Me: What are you thinking?

Tan Tan: Everything all the time.

Me: That kind of thinking will not bring out answers of quality. You have this wonderful gift of being able to think, so you are

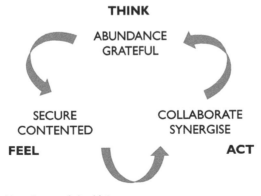

Figure 11.2. Abundance of the Universe
Source: Author

overusing and whipping that gift. Thought chatter interferes with the experience of the present moment, and the present is lost forever. While you are busy judging and ascribing intentions, you might miss an enriching conversation! Thinking is a skill. You have to practise doing it well so it contributes to decision-making, predicting and planning. Stop thinking for a moment!

Tan Tan: No no, can't stop thinking! If I do, I will disappear.

Me: No you won't. For a very long time, the words of the 17th-century French mathematician and philosopher Rene Descartes 'I think, therefore I am' seemed to ring true, but Antonio Damasio pointed out in his book *Descartes Error* that this way of thinking is erroneous (Damasio 1994). Mind and body are deeply intertwined. If you think too much and in various directions, you will burn out the physical cells that make thinking possible. There is no need to fear that reduction in thoughts will turn you into a cabbage. Fears of this kind fuel the epidemic of 'overthinking' and spoil the fun and rewards of thinking productively.

Tan Tan: How do I stop?

Me: Catch yourself and interrupt the chatter. Give your brain something else to do.

Tan Tan: What else can a brain do?

Me: Pay attention to breathing.

Tan Tan: Okay?

Me: Slow down your breathing by holding a breath for four counts. At the next inhalation, feel grateful that the air is here for you to breathe.

Tan Tan: I'm trying, but the OBB is putting its ugly face forward and telling me, 'I can't even do this—can't even breathe how I want to'.

Me: Say this aloud 'I am enough'.

Tan Tan: I am enough.

Me: Louder, OBB can't hear you over all that noise.

Tan Tan: I AM ENOUGH!

Me: How does that work?

Tan Tan: It's stupid and weird to talk to yourself. But it does dent the OBB a little. The buzz is also quietening a little.

Me: Do it often enough to create a new pattern of interruption. When you feel stupid and small, turn the feeling around by wishing a good future to Tan Tan.

Tan Tan: That would be me?

Me: Yes, be nice to Tan Tan; wish him a great future as a Ninja.

Tan Tan: Perhaps you are going cuckoo....

Me: Don't you wish that Tan Tan become the leader of the Ninjas?

Tan Tan: Yes, of course!

Me: Then why can't you wish for yourself what you would wish for a friend?

Tan Tan: Because I am bad and deserve to be disappointed.

Me: I can wish a good future to a bad boy.

Tan Tan: Unh huh... Okay, now I get the hang of this. I wish me well, and I'm feeling better already! What do you call this exercise?

Me: Self-compassion. If you haven't wished good upon yourself, you probably don't know how to wish others well. All the factors that prevent you from experiencing joy, you must decimate one by one. Begin with *fear*. Wish it away. Which *anti-value* is your biggest one?

Tan Tan: Mmm..., I don't want people to laugh at me, and I don't want to give up being a Ninja.

Me: Only your biggest 'don't want' please. If out of the two you mentioned, you could keep only one?

Tan Tan: Ah, I'll keep not wanting to give up being a Ninja!

Me: For keeping that one, you have to let go of the other, so you have to manage your feelings when people do laugh at you. You can do that?

Tan Tan: If it means being able to be the Ninja I always wanted to be, then okay, I can push their sneers aside. This is so cool! I have a 'why' for setting aside my *fear* and *discomfort*.

Me: Now you know what *courage* is.

Tan Tan: Knowing that I have to go past the 'don't want' to get what I really really want!

Me: Now you're talking! Courage is not the absence of fear, but pressing on in spite of fear, knowing something that I truly love is far more important than the discomfort. Next, you have to deal with *guilt*.

Tan Tan: Oh dear! Now I have to tell you the bad stuff I did?

Me: You don't have to tell if you don't want to. Removing blocks in your path to progress is an internal and personal exercise. I am merely a coach, making sure you check all the boxes. The journey is yours.

Tan Tan: The bad thing I did was more than a year ago, but I still feel lousy.

Me: Perhaps you will feel better if you know that guilt visits persons who place a value on being good.

Tan Tan: Now I hate myself! I understand that the feeling comes from the way I think about good and bad. I don't want to change that.

Me: Don't change the basics, but remind yourself that you have already realized that you made a mistake. The bad feeling ensures that you do not repeat the same. Not repeating a similar hurtful act takes some inner adjustment. It involves breaking an old habit or perhaps learning to be more sensitive. When this work is done, guilt can pack up and leave.

> *Nothing ever goes away until it has taught*
> *us what we need to know.*
> —Ani Pema Chödrön

Guilt is like a cuckoo's egg that was laid in your mind when you realized you were bad. The rightful occupant of that mindspace is self-esteem. The cuckoo fledgling grows and kicks the rightful occupant further and further out from the comfortable nest centre and can even topple self-esteem completely out of place.

Tan Tan: Ulp, what do I do? I suppose it was a case of 'hurt people hurt people'. I was hurt and I lashed out. The original hurt still hurts, and then there is this lump of guilt.

Me: Healing old wounds is a responsibility of the wounded individual. You must uncover the old wound and take the required time and care to let it heal. If you don't acknowledge hurt, it remains neglected and festers causing further damage. We have been taught to take care of our body and teeth but did not learn *emotional first aid*. Anytime is a good time to begin.

Tan Tan: The person I lashed out at still holds it against me. I feel I'm in a bad place. Sheesh, this way I will never be a brave leader.

Me: We know that there is work to be done. Try to repair self-esteem from within. Others will find your insecurity and use it to manipulate you and make you jump to their command. A secure personality is the bedrock of leadership, which is not a title or a designation. Leadership is a bunch of qualities that a community looks up to.

Tan Tan: A perfect person?

Me: Tan Tan, no one is perfect. A secure person does not hide her/his imperfections.

Tan Tan: No? Then how will others look up to her/him?

Me: They will see the courage. The courage that it takes to allow others to see you as you are.

Tan Tan: That is too scary! You said that others would see my insecureness and use it to make me jump like at the circus!

Me: They cannot use a flaw that you did not try to hide.

Tan Tan: Oh! Smart move. I save all the energy I use to cover up my scars.

Me: What will you do with the extra energy?

Tan Tan: I will get better at what I do and grow.

Me: When we're not growing, we are not living. All that energy is yours to use for your work. And lots of mindspace!

You could find even more clarity if you learn to process grief, just like you became aware about processing guilt. That is something I need to learn along with you, because as I grow older, I see a lot of broken bridges and shattered dreams. Things that make me sad, empty, angry and desperate.

Tan Tan: I know you lost both your father and mother. It must be hard....

Me: Society allows members to grieve when someone in the family dies. We can even take leave from work on that ground. But we are not allowed to grieve that much if a pet dies, a relationship breaks down, when hope dies or when a dream is shattered. We experience the phenomenon of grief even when a child grows up and the dynamics of the relationship change. It is a physiological process that takes time and adjustment.

Tan Tan: How did relationship get entangled in physiology?

Me: A relationship is a bond, a psycho–neuro–biochemical bond. We internalize a little of the people we build relationships with and identify with our beliefs and dreams. A loss or a breakup is like losing a part of ourselves. We need to heal from the severance. Some people never complete the process of grieving. They rewind and relive the stages of shock, depression, anger, blaming and bargaining, hoping to weld back things as they were imagined to be and recreate the shattered picture within the fancy frame and go into an interminable struggle to recreate what can never be.

Tan Tan: There are stages? Like shock and then sadness?

Me: The order may be different, like anger may come first. Some people are in the habit of blaming, so their thought pattern searches for someone or something to blame. The process can restart a number of times, but if it reaches the stage of acceptance and is processed completely, the person can come out of the mode of grieving. Acceptance is the lever that helps us to flip the track and roll towards healing and return to wholehearted living. It involves cognitive understanding that the loss cannot be reversed, and gradual calming of emotional turbulence that invariably accompanies recall of the topic.

Tan Tan: So, acceptance has stages as well, and it slips into wholesome living. How long does it take once person understands that there's no going back?

Me: The journey from knowing to emotional calm may be a long one.

Tan Tan: Acceptance is not only of loss, it can also be about something new and unusual.

Me: When a new boy joins school and wants to be a part of your friends group, do you accept him immediately?

Tan Tan: No, we check him out first—good points and bad points.

Me: When you decide that he is worthy of including in your group, how do you let him know?

Tan Tan: We pull him into the huddle before we begin a game.

Me: That expanding the huddle and including the new player is what acceptance looks like. We take in a person with all his qualities, good and bad.

Tan Tan: What happens when I am the captain and I know I'm not even good enough to be in the team?

Me: Oh! The saddest feeling is when we cannot and do not accept ourselves.

Tan Tan: I missed three goals in the last match. I disappointed myself!

Me: In a game, you can rest yourself and train, but don't reject yourself from your love. Be generous and kind to yourself, hold out your arms and include yourself in a hug. Be sure that what you will not do for yourself, no one else will do for you. When you disappoint yourself, you grieve the loss of the image you carried of yourself. You can renew your acceptance of self, including all the good and the disappointing stuff.

> *I yearn to be held in the great hands of your heart—*
> *oh let them take me now.*
> *Into them I place these fragments, my life, ...*
> (Excerpts from *I Am Praying Again* by Rainer Maria Rilke)

Tan Tan: In a prayer, a person talks with the God; I thought you would tell me more about accepting my bad for myself.

Me: This excerpt doesn't contain the word 'God', so you can interpret it as a conversation with yourself. The grieving person heals and then opens (the great hands of) her heart to reclaim short bursts of joy and lightness that was impossible while grief reigned.

Tan Tan: 'Fragments' word brings up a broken-glass feeling. What if my Ninja dream gets shattered? My teacher says, 'It's my "fairy tale"'.

Me: In real life, the fairy tales do shatter. A fairy tale has a pre-determined ending. That's why it runs the risk of disappointment. I prefer 'dreams' because dreams don't end and can evolve as life progresses. I encourage you to convert the fairy tale into a dream and work at making it come true. I mean the sort of dream that one dreams while awake. It can be in line with your 'Sense of purpose (USS 13).

Tan Tan: Yes that's the one that I dream while awake—I become a Ninja leader. That's the plan.

Me: Must have a Plan B and a Plan C. No need to be too rigid. It's one thing to be adaptable with the environment, but also wise to be internally adaptable. The Plans B and C will help you cope in case you're disappointed with Plan A falling through.

Tan Tan: You are suggesting that at the start I smell failure. What happened to 'Optimism' of USS 12?

Me: That was a cognitive-level attribute; we have a conscious handle on it. Now we have evidence of the plasticity of neurons; we no longer have an excuse for being brittle in attitude. One has to stay in touch with reality and that can be prickly. See if the attitude position we assume is a viable one. We can check on the thought habits we have developed and see if they work for us or block progress. The ones that are toxic we can try to change, tune down or stop using.

Tan Tan: Thoughts can be toxic? Like poison?

Me: Thoughts and relationships can make us quite ill.

I have Table 11.1 here with some common unhealthy habits and their effects. The way we think affects relationships and quality of relationships also affect health. Business relationships affect the health of careers and finances.

Table 11.1. Thought Habits That Start Out as Useful, Become Toxic When Overused

Thought Habit	Usefulness	Side Effects	Toxic Effects
Comparing and assessing	Accurate assessment of self in relation to others	Stereotyping, judgemental behaviour, competitive behaviour, opinionated and insecure personality	Excessive self-criticism, low self-esteem, depression, low initiative, performance anxiety and relationship problems
Taking on or not accepting responsibility	Accurate accountability and effectiveness	Blame fixing and persecuting (experiences pleasure when someone receives punishment, including self)	Neurosis—blaming self for everything or character disorder—not accepting accountability for anything, poor execution and relationship problems
Anxiety	Predicting pitfalls and taking precautions	Panic attacks, catastrophizing and alarmist behaviour	Sleep disorders, cardiovascular disease, low initiative, no growth and clingy relationships
Obsessive compulsive thinking and circus thinking	Due diligence in research and investigative functions, and perseverance	Perfectionism and stuck in past events	Low output, irritability, health disorders due to eating/washing habits, energy leak and relationship problems

(continued)

(continued)

Thought Habit	Usefulness	Side Effects	Toxic Effects
Drama-centric	Draws attention	Sensationalizing	Low task orientation, embarrasses others, superficial existence and relationship problems
Self-absorption	Self-development	Narcissism and Machiavellian personality	Narcissistic—personality disorder, low empathy and relationship problems
Resentful and unforgiving	Assertion of rights	Indulgent victim play	Energy leak, joylessness, lack of growth and stress-linked diseases
Controlling and manipulative	Management	Aggression, overt or passive, need to be right and opinionated	Frustration due to non-compliance, anger issues and relationship problems
People pleasing	Catering to comforts of others	Can't say 'no' and anxiety	Fatigue, low self-esteem, burnout and related diseases

Source: Author

The phenomenon of neuroplasticity enables each brain to develop differently from any other as it responds to experiences and emotions evoked. The visible product of brain development is a 'personality'. Identical twins raised by the same set of parents attend the same school, go through similar experiences, yet they develop unique characteristics of personality. We may have identical neurons, but they function and connect with each other differently.

The brain is a spatial organ. There are areas in the brain that undertake certain functions, though they are found to be quite plastic and capable of change. It is housed in a limited space (the skull); hence, its growth has to restrict itself.

Like all biological cells and tissues, brain cells obey the 'use it or lose it' principle. The more we use and exercise a certain area and its circuitry, the more robust and efficient the circuit becomes. Some functions are repeated so often that the ease of passage of signals in the circuit is established. The easily conducted actions then no longer demand attention, and we can conduct these activities subconsciously, converting them into habits and skills. Mental activity we do not practise fails to develop, or if previously developed, weakens until exercise is renewed.

An activity that is converted into a habit is executed routinely and invariably, for example, brushing teeth before going to bed. When it is prevented for some reason, there is a generation of discomfort. Mental activity is a product of similar electrical impulses flowing through neuronal circuits. Repeating the activity of thoughts of a certain pattern leads to the development of a 'thought habit'. The thought pattern may manifest as a pattern of behaviour. The individual feels uncomfortable until the full pattern is executed.

Tan Tan: How does a thought pattern end?

Me: Suppose I have a judgemental pattern; it will end when I can pin the blame on someone.

Tan Tan: Mom has a habit of worrying. She never stops.

Me: She may experience some relief by taking action such as by making calls or asking for information.

Tan Tan: Or scolding! And comparing me to my cousin. Now I have a habit of comparing, before she tells me how disappointing I am.

Me: And how does that comparison end up?

Tan Tan: With me feeling like a disappointment. I know, I will never be a Ninja.

Me: That's a very depleting pattern!

Tan Tan: Neuroplasticity, please tell me how I can change it.

Me: It has to stop because it is obstructing you now, though it really began as a motivating tool towards developing competences. You can change it into an empowering new habit by interrupting the pattern and changing track each time you catch yourself indulging. For example, you can catch yourself being judgemental, and you can remind yourself that nobody knows the other person's reality. Perhaps they have a good reason for doing what they do.

Look out of the window at the grassy playground. Do you see the tracks made by the kids who take the shortcut across the grass to the canteen?

Tan Tan: We use it when the gardener is not looking. But yes, the grass doesn't grow there, and we can go faster through it than through the green parts. Raj even takes his bicycle through there, less resistance. I went through there sort of automatically without checking if the gardener was around and got into trouble.

Me: Like that, there are beaten tracks in your brain where the signals are so used to being routed through that we don't even realize we're using them. Some of them are good routes, making work easier, but some of them are counter-productive. Perhaps an overuse of a useful skill like being obsessive about being perfect. I am removed from the present and miss important things going on now. I need to change that because cognitively I know that I can't be perfect but I can bid for my work to be world-class.

Tan Tan: So you find yourself on the beaten track and hop and skip on to an alternate route that will keep you in the present moment?

Me: That route is not so well used, so it will take some walking on to make it efficient and fast.

Tan Tan: Because the only user of the brain is you, no one else is walking on the beaten track and in a while the grass will grow back.

Me: Neuroplasticity made a habit possible to lay down, and the very same principle makes a habit possible to break! The alternatives you provide your brain need to be creative and customized to your life and reward system. Some options that work for a number of people are *mindfulness* and *gratitude*. Interrupt *anxiety* with *gratitude*. Interrupt reminiscing with breathing mindfully and reconnect with the present moment.

Tan Tan: When I catch myself comparing me with others, I will clutch the pebble in my pocket.

Me: Do you have it with you?

[Tan Tan hands me a white pebble about an inch in diameter.]

Me: Here is a marker pen; write on the pebble 'I AM ENOUGH'. By breaking our depleting thought habits and overcoming fear, processing grief to completion and turning expectations into possibilities, we remove the blocks that we had put in our own path. As the negativity recedes, there is room for positive emotion mediators such as endorphins, oxytocin and dopamine to expand the working of the creative processes in the brain.

Tan Tan: Look inside your head, the endorphin said, the team is in dismay, get out of your own way!

> *Knowledge is only a rumor until it lives in the muscle.*
> —Asaro Tribe (Indonesia)

Learning becomes a part of me when it changes the way I react, respond, behave and live.

AT THE BACKDROP
OF ALL 15 USSs

CHAPTER 12

BUILDING RESILIENCE

One of the principal goals of education is to prepare us for failure.
—Stockdale (1984)

Having examined the various patterns and thought habits that turn into obstacles in our own path to self-realization, and learning to get around them, let us turn our attention to building reserve capacity to call upon during hard times.

Tan Tan: If we live the right way, there won't be any hard times!

Me: Which planet are you living on? Plenty of things go wrong on the one I live in. Here, life is unfair and uncertain. It is also interdependent, and what others do and think affect me and vice versa. I'm going to be prepared for traumatic times and make sure that I know how to bounce back.

Tan Tan: Bouncing? Can I bounce even higher than where I started?

Me: I'm sure you can!

Tan Tan: I hope you won't blame me for the crisis when it happens.

Me: When there is a crisis, there isn't much point in pointing fingers. What is required from us is to adapt to the adversity, trauma, tragedy or continued threat, such as health problems or financial stress, and still be capable of contributing to a purpose and using our talents to solve problems and emerge stronger, perhaps wiser.

Tan Tan: I learned about optimism, and I know I will come out
   stronger.
Me: Make sure your brand of optimism is realistic. When you totally
   denied the possibility of hard times, that was 'blind optimism' and
   out of sync with real life.
Tan Tan: Real life is depressing, but you said, it is the only place
   to be. When I live in the past or in my imagination, I miss out
   on what really happened.
Me: If you want to use USS 12 (Optimism) to build resilience, it will
   have to be realistic optimism. These optimists pay close attention
   to the bad news and negative information; they pick out the
   problems they believe can be solved, solve them, create safety
   nets, build lifeboats and then disengage from the negative news
   and motivate themselves and others with the positive possibilities.
   Optimistic motivation makes energy available to power factors
   that boost resilience.

USS 12 (Optimism) derives a lot of strength from USS 3 (Hope/
Faith), although they dwell in very disparate parts of the brain.
Fortifying further is USS 14 (Sense of Power and Control) which
adds the dimension of personal competence, thereby allowing us
to actually believe in ourselves. That is a solidly reliable belief,
much more dependable than faith in mythical powers or belief that
others will save us.

Tan Tan: On the day of the kung fu exam I had to travel 50 km to
   the centre, and a thunderstorm struck at the time I had to leave
   here. The elders said that I could skip the exam and take it after
   six months. No one helped, but I knew I could do it alone.
Me: Why would you want to venture out in a thunderstorm?
Tan Tan: Because I want to become a Ninja as soon as I can. I just
   had to go. But the elders said that it was not as important as an
   academic event, so I could skip it. So, I walked off with an
   umbrella and took the train. On the other side, I had to walk
   some more, but I got to the centre in time and took the exam.

Me: Why did you brave bad weather to take an exam?

Tan Tan: Because I have to qualify and go further. Why are you going 'Why… why… why…'?

Me: All the whys point you to USS 13 (the Spirit of Purpose) that was your motivating factor! To build resilience, we need all the motivating factors we can muster and some coping skills.

There are genetic factors that contribute to capacity for resilience. Some individuals have a genetic variation of the alpha-2-adrenoceptor gene that chemically predisposes to higher levels of baseline norepinephrine, bringing on greater anxiety and slower return to baseline after experiencing stress. This variation makes it hard to bounce back. Another variation occurs in the neuropeptide Y (NPY) gene that lowers the production of NPY, thereby allowing greater activation of the emotional centre (amygdala) during threat perception and inadequate inhibition of norepinephrine release, making it difficult to restore calm after the perception of threatening conditions has passed. These genetic variations result in a hyperactive stress response system that manifests as incapacitating anxiety and a susceptibility to post-traumatic stress disease.

The stress response is essential to living creatures, activating rapidly in response to threat, enough to take action to respond appropriately to danger, saving lives and deactivating as soon as the danger has passed. During the heightened sense of danger (USS 6), the processes of creative thought and ideation are left out of the circuit in order to facilitate rapid response to imminent danger. Emotional regulation training involves inserting a pause in the reaction just long enough to allow the decision-making intelligent forebrain to connect and contribute. This pause is just half a second in duration and allows the individual to perform intelligently under pressure.

Tan Tan: Then I can have the use of my thinking brain, even though I'm in trouble!

Me: Resilient people have access to both emotion and reason to make decisions using both the PFC and the vital value-linked information from the limbic system (emotions and memory).

Tan Tan: Why can't I switch off the threat response? It triggers even when I'm not facing death. Like when the elder is frowning—I just can't think!

Me: Response to threat is essential for survival. Nature will not allow it to be turned off. The consequence of the threat response is stress, which is necessary for the growth of competence, strength and wisdom. Why else did Prince Siddhartha leave the comforts of the palace?

Tan Tan: To learn and grow. Not learning is like not living! One senior monk has a very angry expression. When that face is around, I can't seem to pay attention. Must be the threat response hijack. I don't see why he has to be angry with a sincere boy like me.

Me: And so awfully cute! Come on, you said that you would swap your entitled attitude for a grateful one!

Tan Tan: I have rights.

Me: It stops there. The world does not owe us anything, though we keep helping ourselves to the planet's resources. A delusion of being entitled to special perks leads to a lot of complaining and victimhood, and certainly does not help in building capacity to withstand adversity.

Tan Tan: Okay, then what does build capacity?

Me: Make sure that you are fit and strong—both mentally and physically. Physical training resets the autonomic nervous system to anticipate a sudden demand. Training slows the heart rate, lowers blood pressure and improves heart rate variability. Exercise lowers the risk of fractures, improves cognition, memory and attention. The planning and decision-making required in sports reduce threat response through hours of practice and preparatory tournaments, ensuring that the trainee is thoroughly prepared and pre-tested. The body develops familiarity with conditions of a high heart rate, sweating and fatigue (similar to panic) in the relatively safe environment of the sports field; such familiarity is practice for the interoceptive interpretation, which tunes itself not to interpret these somatic markers as dangerous or life-threatening, but more as excitement. Gradual increments in exercise, with the celebration of achievements, help to build self-esteem and perseverance.

Tan Tan: Bring it on, I'm ready for anything!

Me: Sport is also competitive. As long as competition is maintained in a healthy manner, it enhances performance and pushes us to achieve what we may not, had we felt unchallenged. It gives individuals the opportunity to taste the emotions of winning and losing, and to manage these with grace. The competitive nature of academic grading and assessment also fulfils the training criteria for resilience building, but occasionally competition grows ugly and failure is viewed as punitive and akin to brutal rejection, causing deep wounds in self-worth.

Coaches, parents and mentors must make themselves aware about fine-tuning challenge to the tolerance level of the individual and gradually tighten the challenge to bring each one to peak performance. When pushed too hard, the subject displays signs of irritation, anxiety and later panic, whereas if there is inadequate challenge applied, the player is slack and inattentive.

Tan Tan: The swimming coach made me so angry yesterday, I pushed a girl off the edge because she was giggling while he scolded me!

Me: Oh no! Tan Tan, we get angry only when norepinephrine is secreted in the body. You must take responsibility for what goes on inside your skin. It is for you to navigate the emotion and manage your neurotransmitters. No one else can do that for you.

Tan Tan: [*Tears welling up in his eyes*] I miss Mom, she could kiss my pain away. She was not inside my skin, but she could change my chemistry.

Me: Her love and gentleness brought out oxytocin. The body usually prefers the peaceful hormones. When the feel-good hormones are at work, the feel-bad chemicals get cleared away. You are growing up now, Mom can't be with you all the time. You must take charge of yourself and take responsibility for your emotional chemistry.

Tan Tan: [*Squaring his shoulders*] Yeah. Have to be a Ninja!

Me: Be gentle and loving to yourself, and trust yourself to regulate spikes of emotions by yourself. Allow yourself to experience the full range of feel-good and feel-bad, and choose a baseline mood to return to after a deviation. Make sure you respect yourself by getting in touch with what you are willing to stand up for and against.

Tan Tan: Stop stop! You're making my mind buzz.

Me: You can't blame me for your mental indiscipline. You are the owner of the mind and the only user. Use it well. When you overthink, the mind begins to use you. You must stay in charge.

Tan Tan: Is it okay to not feel okay occasionally?

Me: All the emotions are useful. Take fear as an example. Fear is energizing. It prepares us to take appropriate action to avert danger. The rush of catecholamines (epinephrine/adrenaline) it releases enhances the alacrity of the thinking cortex, though very high levels cause short-circuit reaction and leave the intelligent processes offline.

If you have not experienced all the levels, you do not know how to navigate your path and retain control. You also know how you like to feel and can choose activities that take you to that level. People who feel they are not in charge of even their own equipment, tend to give up easily. Ninjas don't give up. If they face a setback, they recoup and bounce back into action.

THE RESILIENCE TRAINING KIT

In resilience training, there are things to learn and things to unlearn.

Tan Tan: Unlearn?

Me: Unlearn as in look at things differently, one word for that is 'reappraise', and break the old pattern of thought and action that are toxic or just leaking away energy and perhaps occupying chunks of mindspace. Like the habit of comparing, stereotyping and presuming. There is also the problem of giving far too much importance to what other people are thinking about you. Since there are many components in the resilience training kit, I put it in the form of Table 12.1. To begin, review your attitude towards failure.

Table 12.1. Elements of Building Resilience

Use Intrinsic Ability (Based on One or More USSs)	Learn/Do More of/ Do Better	Unlearn/Stop Doing/Reappraise
Self-assessment	Extract learning from failure and grow	Lowering self-worth due to failure
Secure personality	Accurate assessment of own competence (humility)	Distorted assessment and ego imbalance
Introspection	Facing fear	Shame, secrecy
Optimism	Positive reappraisal	Helplessness
	Realistic optimism	Pessimism
Time management	Clear goals and priorities	Procrastination, people pleasing and chasing other's goals in order to fit in
Inner adaptability	Acceptance and forgiving	Denial
Recognize the right thing	Recognize values and purpose, appreciate privilege	Entitlement and take for granted

Use Intrinsic Ability (Based on One or More USSs)	Learn/Do More of/ Do Better	Unlearn/Stop Doing/Reappraise
Expectations	Open to possibilities	Rigid and pre-determined
Emotional regulation	Respond after consideration, appropriate delaying of gratification, frustration tolerance	React on impulse
Responsibility	Take on tasks within the circle of influence and be accountable for them	Take on all or none of the blame
Faith	In own competence and on goodness and abundance	Superstition and blackmailing of higher powers
Knowledge	Curiosity	Being right
Environmental adaptability	Adaptability with the present and preparation for the future	Rigidity and control
Problems	Problem focus and task orientation, celebration of milestones	Avoidance/ catastrophizing
Empathy	Compassion	Judgement
Humour	Detect the funny side	Sarcasm and cynicism
Interpersonal tension	Conflict resolution and collaboration	Harbouring resentment
Relationship management	Interdependence in relationships	Exploitative relationships

Source: Author

Me: Thanks to the phenomenon of neuroplasticity, the very processes that help us to learn and master a skill and are also involved in weakening the detrimental practices we have developed over time.

Tan Tan: I hear the word 'humility' over and over again at the monastery discourses. I have no clue about what it means.

Me: I watched the basketball practice session yesterday. The coach asked the players to stand in single file according to shoulder height. I noticed that the players kept hustling each other and arguing. Someone ran off to bring a card and tape measure, and the simple task took double the time it actually needed.

Tan Tan: [*Giggling*] That happens every time. The boys are all growing you know.

Me: Though height is not a competence, it is assessed using a tape measure. But for assessing some competence parameters, we use 'Sense of Power and Control' (USS 14). The lure of overassessment is strong because when I expand my sense of abilities and influence, it feels very good. Ego balance is a dynamic and continuous process of keeping the assessment on the dot. The dot is called the point of humility. Neither too high nor too low—just accurate.

Tan Tan: See that's why I get confused. What the monks say makes me think that 'humility' means keeping myself small.

Me: They put it that way because most people fall for the lure of feel-good associated with over assessing. I warn people about underassessing because that paralyzes us. So, can we settle for the 'accurate' assessment of competence as a definition for humility?

Tan Tan: Another balancing act? How does humility figure in building resilience?

Me: An accurate assessment about your own abilities and social position is the base upon which the personality performs. A well-balanced ego makes a stable base (secure base) for the personality. Dealing with criticism and setbacks becomes easy because ego size is pre-adjusted and no alteration is required.

Tan Tan: I understood that facing my fears will help me to be brave, but what is this about 'unlearning shame and secrecy'? I don't want to announce things about me that I am ashamed about.

Me: What will happen when others know your shameful secret?

Tan Tan: They may stop being friends with me.

Me: I guess, they are now friends with Tan Tan minus his shame. That is not all of Tan Tan. Is the whole Tan Tan (warts and all) not worthy of their friendship?

Tan Tan: Perhaps, if they knew the whole story, some of them would move away but a few may stay as friends. Doesn't everyone have something to be ashamed about?

Me: What if we stopped hiding our flaws?

Tan Tan: Mmm... That would push away the shallow friendships and leave me only more genuine friends, and (breathing deeply) much more relaxed! But it would be hard to become all see-through and transparent. Feels sort of scary!

Me: Living openly and transparently requires courage. It is the only way to live if we want to live wholeheartedly and completely. Courage becomes available to us when we are clear about what we value and what we are willing to take risks for. If you are proud of your values and purpose, why would you hide them? Such open transparent lives are the ones that inspire others.

Tan Tan: I dare because I care.

> *Without courage, all virtue is fragile: admired, sought after, professed, but held cheaply and surrendered without a fight.*
>
> —John Mc Cain, a politician

Me: We even need to be open to ourselves. When I do the naming of values exercise with my students, I come across a mismatch between 'professed values' and 'practised values'. We get quite good at pretending to ourselves. We free up a lot of energy when we decide to stop playing the game.

Tan Tan: Maybe they got so used to hiding from others that they can no longer see themselves. They are lying about themselves to others and to themselves! That could feel better than looking at your own imperfection?

A young man who came to me to coach with the aim of rescuing his marriage, let's call him Akshay, named 'relationship' as his primary value (what he cares about the most). The real story was that whenever he argued with his wife, he would not speak to anyone at home, not even his five-year-old daughter for weeks. It was pointed out to him that this behaviour demonstrated that what he really cared most about was safeguarding his ego, and though he professed his love for the family, he subjected them to his mood display and dissatisfaction instead of taking initiative to address the cause and mend the relationship. He digested the external point of view over some days and gradually worked on his role in the relationship, which is what made a significant impact and completely turned around the life and satisfaction levels of the three persons.

Tan Tan: I'm worried about the five-year-old girl. Adults need to sort themselves out before becoming parents. Akshay believed that he was a loving dad? The little girl must be so confused!

Me: Sense of self is strong, but self-awareness has to be practised. Being honest with oneself is as difficult as allowing others to see our flaws. Only when I accept that I have a problem, the option to try and get better opens up. When I create a shell of pretension around me, others cannot see me as I am, and I cannot see the real world too clearly from inside the shell either.

Tan Tan: Uh oh! Got to come out of that egg shell. I'm not ready yet, but real life does seem rather interesting. Problems inside my head and problems outside phew!

Me: Perhaps you are ready to view difficulty outside of yourself as challenge?

Tan Tan: Isn't that how Prince Siddhartha began? By taking on the jungle beasts first? Okay, I can keep the inside awareness for later. Right now, I have a tough math problem and have to submit a project proposal to work on during the holidays. Suppose I look long and hard at the math problem; I can try to use it to get an idea for the project work. It will be original!

Me: [*Surprised but pretending not to be*] Being able to see opportunity in adversity is a product of positive reappraisal. A proactive and advanced level of optimism.

[Tan Tan has detected the admiration in my tone.]

Tan Tan: Thanks, I learn fast and adapt quickly. My teacher told us that Charles Darwin said those who adapt will survive.

Me: Adaptability is important for resilience building too, and it includes internal adaptability.

Tan Tan: Internal? Yes, I can adapt to your style of cooking because I like food from all parts of the world.

Me: I mean inwardly accepting what cannot be changed, even though I don't like it. It also involves forgiving those who hurt you or forgiving yourself for a big mistake.

Tan Tan: Ulp, that's harder than adapting to discomfort and alien food. I can't forgive my parents for sending me off to the monastery. My brother and sister are still at home. I will always hold it against them.

Me: How does your resentment help anyone? Wasn't there a reason?

Tan Tan: Yes, they were poor and still are. I sometimes get tired of holding on to my grudge but don't know why I hold on to it.

Me: As a Ninja, you will need all the energy you can get. How much do you think the grudge is taking up? On a scale of 10, how much energy does it take to keep the resentment going?

Tan Tan: Not much, just 1 out of 10.

Me: For the whole lifetime that adds up to a lot of wasted energy. Another Ninja of your size will have all 10 of 10 available for the competition to top spot.

Tan Tan: Oh! But my parents don't deserve to be forgiven!

Me: The energy leak is yours, Tan Tan.

Tan Tan: [*Grrr*] Okay, I will get around to forgiving someday. I get so mad each time I think about this.

Me: That will eat up some more in terms of focus. When you are angry, how much of the attention pie does the anger take up? In percentage points?

Tan Tan: Gnash gnash... a full 100 per cent.

Me: A Ninja has to give 100 per cent attention to fight evil; you can't afford to relive the anger of the past. When forgiveness is complete, recalling the matter is no longer accompanied by the resurgence of the feel-bad. You will need all the attention you can gather.

Tan Tan: [*Scowling*] They are BAD parents!

Me: Situations that you don't approve of need to be changed through solutions, not merely condemned, criticized and cursed.

Tan Tan: I can't change what they have already done! They were poor and they kept having more kids. How can one small Tan Tan change the big stupid world?

Me: You could learn your lessons well and create a project for changing what you don't like about the world, using all your fresh education. As you go along, you can gather support or chip away at the problem bit by bit. Being angry and resentful will deplete energy and focus. Both are finite resources.

Tan Tan: How can I forgive? How do I even start?

Me: Try to feel their difficulties and then wish them a healthy fulfilling life.

Tan Tan: I already know how difficult life is at home. I feel it every time; I think about them. And you want me to wish that they have a good or least a better life? [*Closing his eyes*] Okay, wishing them a good life wasn't too difficult! Mmm…, it feels good too, sort of light and floaty! What is this exercise called?

Me: Empathy and compassion. Empathy is intrinsic, and we named it USS 5, so it happens quite subconsciously. To be compassionate, we have to use imagination and thought. It happens in all awareness at the higher centres. When we exercise compassion, it is something that we do intentionally; it works like meditation.

Tan Tan: A wish for someone else which ends up making me feel good! The elder says meditation is good for my immunity, and I will stay healthy if I do more of it.

Me: When you're having a hard time, if you can wish those persons who are giving you a hard time a good life, progress and wellness, when you do bounce out of the hard times, you will still be healthy! Not just wishing but participating in activity that will be good for/useful to others is also good for us.

Tan Tan: Really? What is that exercise called?

Me: Altruism. But we drifted away from learning how to forgive.

Tan Tan: You were saying that to forgive is intentional or does it happen over time?

Me: It is a particularly difficult form of acceptance and need not have any external indications. We don't have to advertise. It's far too personal and mainly for our own good. Altruistic action towards self, letting go of a grudge.

Tan Tan: Quietly forgive. What then?

Me: Now work together side by side. The undisputable wisdom of evolution has blessed us with a system that rewards us intrinsically via the nucleus accumbens each time we act in cooperation with other creatures.

Tan Tan: I can feel smug enough when I get something all for myself.

Me: When we behave selfishly, we can intellectually appreciate the benefit to self, but the behaviour fails to trigger the intrinsic feeling of elevation and pride.

Tan Tan: Working together could get us out of the hard times quicker.

Me: Nice to have some company when the going gets rough! When do sailors need a lifeboat?

Tan Tan: When there's a storm at sea and the big ship may turn over or crack open.

Me: When and where are lifeboats built? During a storm out at sea?

Tan Tan: No. Right here on land on a sunny day, when all is well. That is when a Ninja practices his art.

Me: That's when resilience training is done.

Tan Tan: When I'm in the middle of a storm, I really can't tell how big it is.

Me: At such a time, you could use a sufficiently well-developed USS 10, the one that helps us to move from the delusion of being central to the Universe and gives perspective. You use your angular gyrus to help you zoom out and look at yourself and your problems from a distance. That way you get an idea of how big things are in relation to each other and to the Universe. That perspective helps you make effective decisions. An easy way is to imagine you changed places with that fly on the wall and got a 360-degree view of Tan Tan throwing a tantrum.

Tan Tan: Ah I can do that! What do you call this exercise?

Me: Spirituality.

Tan Tan: Are you sure?

Me: Zoom out and look at you. Be a witness to yourself. See where you stand in relation to the world. That's my definition of spirituality. I won't push it down your throat; you can come up with your own explanation. When you do, we can review the name for this exercise. I'm putting it all in a table so that you can see how USSs we have numbered 1–15 are used to build resilience (Table 12.2). They can participate as motivators, facilitators or coping skills.

Table 12.2. Role of USSs in Resilience Building

USS No.	Name	Role in Resilience Building
1.	Consciousness and Sense of Self	Maintaining self-worth. [*Motivating factor*]
2.	Sense of Belonging	Basis for secure personality. [*Facilitator*]
3.	Sense of Hope aka Faith	Cultivating belief in self. [*Motivating factor*]
4.	Emotion	Self-regulation contributes to belief in self, leveraging energy released by fear and anger, focus on immediate action and deactivation of stress at appropriate time. [*Motivating factor and coping skill*]
5.	Empathy	Bonding, basis for cooperation and relationship building. [*Facilitator*]
6.	Pain and Threat Perception	Ego balance/humility. [*Motivating factor*]
7.	Interoception	Mindfulness, gratitude, presence, contributes to clarity in thought and access to wisdom, and value-based decisions. [*Facilitator*]

(continued)

(continued)

USS No.	Name	Role in Resilience Building
8.	Position and Balance	Developing grace and intellectual balance. [*Facilitator*]
9.	Sense of Passage of Time	Effectiveness and efficiency. [*Facilitator*]
10.	Sense of Proportion	Accurate assessment of self in the perspective of others and the Universe, and spirituality. [*Facilitator*]
11.	Sense of Fairness	Objectivity and justice. [*Motivating factor*]
12.	Optimism	Perseverance in the face of obstacles and setback. [*Motivating factor*]
13.	Purpose	Goal directedness and prevents dissipation of energy. [*Motivating factor*]
14.	Power and Control	Accurate assessment of competencies. [*Facilitator*]
15.	Sense of Humour	Bonding, conflict management and stress reduction. [*Coping skill*]

Source: Author

Tan Tan apparently doesn't care for tables like Table 12.2. He is waving cheerily at friends passing my window.

Tan Tan: Hey Arjun, catch you after class in the canteen today.
Me: Ahem. Can we get back to resilience building?
Tan Tan: Do friends count? Mine make me feel stronger.
Me: Quality relationships surely count in our ability to bounce back. Even the relationship we have with our doctors counts in our recovery from illness. What is at work is the magic hormone of bonding—oxytocin.
Tan Tan: You don't seem to have too many friends. To make friends, you have to 'be' a friend.

> *You can make more friends in 2 months by becoming*
> *interested in other people, than you can in 2 years*
> *by trying to get other people interested in you.*
>
> —Dale Carnegie

Me: Oh, I have some wonderful and inspiring friends! Resilient and bouncy people who have grappled with disease, disability, lawsuits, harassment, loss and abuse.

Tan Tan: Wow! Can I meet them? Did they bounce back stronger?

Me: Yes, they live exemplary lives. They are role models, and looking at them we see what resilience looks like and we can aspire to build that quality within ourselves. They emerged from their tribulations with something extra called wisdom.

Even if a great personality is not personally known to us, we can still model our development on their example. They show us the way. We call them 'heroes'.

Resilience in a person cannot be proved until tested, but a sign of well-developed resilience is seen as 'grace'.

Tan Tan: That's a new word. Is it an exercise?

Me: Grace is visible as an openness—an authentic presence that enables us to face what is happening, calmly and courageously. It is the visible component of the confidence that comes from resilience and knowledge of invisible boundaries that are known through the use of wisdom.

Tan Tan: Grace is not an exercise but the result of all the exercises we talked about.

Me: We could learn more about resilience from James Bond Stockdale, the former Vice Admiral of the US Navy and a veteran from the war in Vietnam, who spent over seven years as a prisoner of war. The experience of war is frequently a cause of severe scarring of the psyche, but a few individuals come out stronger, with their sanity intact and richer for the experience in terms of wisdom. Stockdale advises:

You must not confuse faith that you will prevail in the end
(which you can never afford to lose) with the discipline to
confront the most brutal facts of your current reality,
whatever they might be.

CHAPTER 13
HOW TO TRAIN A NINJA: DEVELOPING AUTHENTIC RESILIENT LEADERSHIP

Tan Tan has fallen asleep. I'll be very quiet so his brain can recuperate by shrinking its myriad synapses. This winding down makes room for new learning. Young people often forgo sleep to be able to learn well, but that is counter-productive. Awareness and timely guidance are central to optimal brain development. The more the awareness amongst teachers and parents, the earlier guided development can begin. Leadership development begins in the home with many opportunities for parents to help children address and navigate their emotions. Exercises in restraint and delaying of gratification can start right there. The affection styles of parents have a lasting impression on a child, so parenting with awareness about the secure style nurtures a generation of secure personalities. Kindergarten is a great place to spot and develop empathy, and the sports field is a cradle for a healthy teamwork and sporting spirit. College is a setting for lessons in bonding with and influencing others, and executive trainers have the opportunity to reinforce the emotional reality of both individuals and teams, hitherto brushed under office carpeting.

Emotions have been retained through eons of natural selection. A newborn comes into existence fully equipped to sense and express contentedness and discomfort. It is only ignorance that prevents the Acknowledgement of emotional intelligence. Today we know more because new imaging technology has made the working of the living brain visible through fMRI and positron emission tomography scans. Access to results of research can translate into timely interventions for the sake of executive and leadership development.

Because we now know more about the impact of the environment in developing attitudes and we know that some attitudes are toxic to the person harbouring them, I feel a deep sadness when I come across cases of self-harm and failure to realize immense potential. Often parents who believe they know what is best for their children are the ones who are responsible for nurturing self-destructive attitudes and thought habits. Similarly, teachers, coaches or other persons in positions of power are known to decimate the self-worth of individuals to pulp, not knowing that their handling of adolescents and young adults leads them to spiral into depression, self-harm and suicide.

A case that generated such sadness is that of an immensely bright boy whose brilliance and repartee made his father feel small. The father used every opportunity available to put the boy 'in his place'. That place proved to be at the bottom of the class, far behind his peers in social conduct and political awareness.

Here is another case.

An IT professional who apparently had everything going for her. She had a job, a husband and wealthy families on both sides. Yet she behaved self-destructively and indulged in reckless behaviour after frequent quarrels with family members. The reckless risk-taking behaviour earned her a label of being 'mad' following which she had nothing to lose and quite enjoyed creating a nuisance for the family. These are the people who pushed her towards an arranged marriage only because she was close to 30 years old. When asked why she was against the marriage, she did not speak, too afraid to spell out her dream of being an entrepreneur before an audience known to scoff and ridicule her point of view.

These are brilliant people who have been labelled as 'crazy', medicated and dulled into zombies. Their fault being that they had a potential that the persons around them found intimidating.

These individuals had to be taken away from the relationship dynamics to repair the damage done. The 30-year-old girl was able to isolate herself by taking admission in a foreign university for higher studies. When allowed to heal self-worth and regain confidence by freeing her from chasing other people's goals, there was no looking back. Other young people from her town look up to her as she shines like a dazzling supernova, an international 'Block Chain' consultant. Something no one in her town had ever heard of.

Tan Tan: She doesn't know that she is a leader and lots of young people are following her! That's a nice way to be. Glad, you're writing about leadership today.

Me: [*Sigh*] So, you're awake? Yes, I'm only writing about applying neurology research results to leadership development. Creatures that live in groups, as humans do, organize themselves in societies.

Every such entity (collective of creatures) craves leadership for the benefit of the collective. The smallest collective in our case is the unit of family. Notice how the established norm of patriarchy places the father unquestioningly on the throne of leadership. That is merely a designation. All members take up leadership roles as and when situations that demand their expertise arise.

Tan Tan: Those examples you mentioned reminded me that leadership begins in the family. People need to qualify to have the privilege of becoming parents.

Me: Parenting is a bigger responsibility than we expect. I wish we could get all prospective parents and teachers to take the pledge, at least do no harm. Parents and mentors, see Table 13.1 and note that what we want to teach young people in addition to their academic curriculum are known as Executive Functions. The teaching, mostly by example, gets coded in pathways within the brain in specific locations mentioned in the right column of the table. These are the muscles that require exercise and training.

Tan Tan: Even a king like Siddhartha's dad was pushing him in the wrong direction. Hundreds of years later, the world respects the Buddha and no one remembers the dad.

Me: In a progressively flattening world, where designation fails to strike awe and subjugation, the need to value 'leadership' and what works becomes imperative.

Tan Tan: What about people like you who work alone? I don't suppose that you need leadership skills.

Me: I 'lead' a life, don't I? Leadership begins as the inside job of discipline.

Table 13.1. Executive Functions with Related Brain Structures That Enable Them

Executive Functions	Related Brain Structure
Emotional memory	Amygdala (limbic system)
Response to emotional turmoil	Right pre-frontal cortex
Decision for appropriate response	Left pre-frontal cortex
Soothing of emotions	Orbito-frontal cortex

(continued)

(continued)

Executive Functions	Related Brain Structure
Delaying gratification	Orbito-frontal cortex
Bringing subconscious emotions to level of cognition	Insular cortex
Access to intuition	Right interior insular cortex
Finding anomalies and mistakes	Right pre-frontal cortex
Negativity	Right pre-frontal cortex
Seeing opportunity	Left pre-frontal cortex
Motivation to keep trying in face of setback	Left pre-frontal cortex
Ability to turn around negative mood	Left pre-frontal cortex
Empathy	Mirror cells scattered in many brain areas especially in anterior cingulate cortex, insula and limbic system
Creativity and ideation	Right hemisphere
Mindfulness and attention to task	Left hemisphere

Source: Author

Tan Tan: My plan is to be the best at martial arts. Being the best will give me the leader's spot.

Me: Being the best technically may get you the spot, but you will find it hard to maintain the position, because what counts when you are in the spot are other competencies—those in the emotional competencies framework, notably political awareness, conflict management and inspiring people.

Leaders have to be accepted by those who they lead. Leadership acceptance depends on whether people look up to you. One becomes eligible for the position only after cultivating enduring qualities like presence, transparency and resilience.

Tan Tan: I remember that resilience has to be built like a lifeboat, but I'm not comfortable with transparency, especially as a warrior.

Me: Others who accept you in the position of a leader will be watching you all the time, looking for a mismatch between what you say and do, wondering whether to trust you.

Tan Tan: I will be a master in martial arts by then; they better trust me!

Me: If they find you are not too proficient, they may forgive you, but not if there is a gap between the values you profess and those you practise. Which is why I suggest you take some time over the exercise of verbalizing your values and start by being honest to yourself. Others can easily observe the values you practise, though you may be fooling yourself with your 'should' and 'supposed to' tinted glasses.

People will sniff out your intentions through instinctive perception that works through mirror neurons. The perception (USS 5, Empathy) may well be completely subconscious and instantaneous and allows us to read feelings and intentions of others, and occasionally what they're thinking.

Tan Tan: Uh oh! So they know if I think they're irritating?

Me: You can bet on that. A leader's list of must haves is presence, transparency and resilience.

Tan Tan: And how does one have presence?

Me: You could start by paying attention. Complete unadulterated attention. You know that attention is focus, and if you are in the throes of a negative emotion, focus is directed to the problem and not available for you to give to other people.

Tan Tan: I could give *some* attention....

Me: You will be only partly present. I want my leaders to be fully present and completely attentive. What you can *do* is *listen* like each person is the only person in the world.

Tan Tan: Come on! You know how many people there are in my life?

Me: No half-measures. Full attention is the same as full respect. You cannot give respect by withholding attention. That is the only way to convey that the person has been seen as well as heard. Listen with your eyes, ears and your whole body speaking the language of attentiveness. If you want to know what else you can *do*, ask the people you lead. Ask what you can *do* for them. Then *do* that.

Tan Tan: When do I get some me time? When can I be myself?

Me: When you are transparent, you are you all the time. Transparent is light. Pretending is tedious, like wearing a suit of armour is exhausting. Open people can have fun on the job. Fun is good, goes well with leadership!

Tan Tan: What about my needs? I'm only human. All leaders are humans?

Me: Then you must remember that everyone is human and has the usual basic needs. As a leader, you must acknowledge these needs and make sure that people have what they need. Make sure that they feel included and significant. Acknowledge their anger; be grateful that they care enough to feel. Give them freedom to align individual aspirations with team objectives. Provide clear directions with opportunities to grow and learn. Let them participate in the vision and mission of the group.

Tan Tan: I can't allow people to be angry....

Me: You can't stop people from feeling or thinking. People get angry when they care about something. You must acknowledge and thank them for caring enough to be angry. Anger makes energy available to change what we are unhappy about. A leader guides the efficient use of that energy.

Needs are biological; we have discussed this in Chapter 3 (summarized in Table 3.1). We can't beat evolutionary design. We can learn how to function best within the scope the design and architecture of the brain allows.

Tan Tan: The design has limitations.

Me: I agree, but the existing design is non-negotiable.

Tan Tan: I will use technology to make up for the existing limitations. I will be all powerful... Ha... ha... ha!

Me: Growing power does feel good!

[Tan Tan is goose-stepping around the room holding both arms out wide, taking up a lot of room and threatening to knock over my porcelain souvenirs. He is still going 'ha... ha... ha'.]

Me: Tch... tch—hubris brings down the best. I worry about you, Tan Tan. Here read this table from bottom up.

[I'm getting worried and looking up my notes from Jim Collin's book *Good to Great*. In this book, Collins has outlined five levels of leadership, and while making notes I added emotional competence requirements and created Table 13.2.]

Table 13.2. Emotional Competence Demanded from Leaders of Five Levels

Level of Leadership	Name	Description	Emotional Competence Requirements
5	Executive	Builds enduring greatness	Subjugates ego (transcends self) and transfers it to team + resonance + emotional intelligence
4	Effective leader	Stimulates people to achieve high performance	Ego + alignment of organizational and individual goals (resonance) + emotional intelligence
3	Competent manager	Organizes people to achieve pre-determined objectives	Ego + self-regulation and relationship management (emotional intelligence)
2	Contributing team member	Works with others effectively in group setting	Ego + interpersonal effectiveness
1	Capable individual	Contribute through talent, knowledge, skills	Individual ego is a driving force

Source: Collins (2001)

[Tan Tan stops the evil laughter routine and takes a look.]

Tan Tan: The requirement expands as we go upwards.

Me: Notice that ego features strongly in the lower rungs. Ego is a potent driving force and cannot be left out. But at the topmost level, to transition from *effective* to *great*, hinges on an ability to rise above the individual ego and transfer pride and power perception over to the team.

Tan Tan: Oh! I have to share?

Me: Share credit. The performance of the team becomes your legacy and not your individual achievements.

Tan Tan: Legacy? I work hard and become a Ninja leader and you want me to think about leaving? Why would I leave? Then I become a nobody!

Me: Relax! There's no danger of losing your greatness if you practise *equanimity*, *poise* and never stop *learning*. Persons who have established these qualities within continue to inspire others even when they step away from the designated official status.

Tan Tan: Like retire? You mean the power to lead remains? Does that sort of power have a name?

Me: Influence without authority.

Tan Tan: Sounds like there's more to training to be a Ninja leader than martial art practice. How do I train to get that sort of power that comes without designation?

Me: Start right now. You can play games that strengthen specific brain pathways.

Tan Tan: Like a brain gym? Do they have these?

Me: You won't require a special place. These exercises can be tried anywhere: at home, at school, in the playground, in office....

Tan Tan: Do I have to pass an entrance test?

Me: When you see what the activities are, you will know that you have already enrolled, not knowing that there is a brain circuit doing push-ups in the background. Some of it can look easy or silly. See Table 13.3 given on next page.

Table 13.3. Leadership Competencies and (with) Exercises to Strengthen Them

Competence to Be Exercised (A)	Self-Control
Brain structures involved	Prefrontal cortex (PFC) and orbito-frontal cortex (OFC)

Suggested activity (life will be generous with opportunities to practice these)	1. Exercises in delaying gratification:
	    (a) Delay watching the movie till an assignment is complete
	    (b) Delay intimacy till the third date
	2. Anger management practice:
	    (a) Use incidents that anger you to get familiar with the physiological turmoil anger creates
	    (b) Create a pause strategy to enable a considered response
	3. Games: Play statue; Play suzz—a number of people make a circle and call out consecutive numbers, say 'buzz' in place of multiples of any number (e.g., 5)
	4. Take on adventure trips and camping; practise adapting to unusual circumstances

Introspective activity	1. What was I looking for in that angry incident? (Refer Chapter 3, Page 27) 2. Think up a more appropriate response than the one you displayed 3. Find something funny in the incident 4. Awareness about needs in self and in others 5. Congratulate yourself each time you are successful in exercising restraint
Competence to Be Exercised (B)	Empathy/Interpersonal Effectiveness
Brain structures involved	Multiple structures involving mirror neurons
Suggested activity	1. Social awareness 2. Encourage exposure to various cultures 3. Exercises in observation, attention to detail 4. Try to mimic body language, pace, gait of a group and integrate as a new entrant 5. Try out alien cuisine along with the style and ambience

(continued)

(continued)

Competence to Be Exercised (B)	Empathy/Interpersonal Effectiveness
Introspective activity	1. Appreciate diverse customs and viewpoints 2. Exercise tolerance 3. Get curious about customs and rituals 4. Disallow judgemental critical thoughts

Competence to Be Exercised (C)	Self-confidence
Brain structures involved	Multiple structures, mainly left PFC
Suggested activity	1. Take on any opportunity for public speaking and high visibility 2. Practise skills to achieve proficiency (mastery) in a chosen field 3. Take mock interviews 4. Video record a performance and play it back; see what you want to improve
Introspective activity	1. Become aware of the incremental rise in ease of conducting the task 2. Imagine the level of ease you aspire to achieve 3. Congratulate yourself on the slightest improvement

Competence to Be Exercised (D)	Transparency and Trust Generation
Brain structures involved	Mirror neuron exercise and awareness
Suggested activity	1. Play dumb charade 2. Watch films with sound muted or foreign film with no subtitles and try to guess the story 3. Keep every small promise you make, especially to yourself and close friends 4. Practise punctuality 5. Practise active listening 6. Learn about body language
Introspective activity	1. Appreciate the way your body feels when you attune to another person and feel the emotional state of another by mirroring and paying attention 2. Become aware about fears and inadequacy, guilt and shame 3. Process these (take professional's help if required)

Competence to Be Exercised (E)	Intuitiveness
Brain structures involved	Insula
Suggested activity	1. Describe how the body feels during certain mood and emotion; learn to detect these early 2. Name emotions (emotional literacy) 3. Draw emoticons 4. Practise breathing exercises 5. Learn and practise mindfulness during routine actions like walking/eating 6. Practice self-talk 7. Listen to your body
Introspective activity	Become aware about change in energy levels with different situations and interpret the meaning. Energized feeling comes with prospects aligned with what we truly care about. Depleted feeling comes with the prospects that frighten us or feel wrong.
Competence to Be Exercised (F)	**Ego Balance/Humility**
Brain structures involved	Integrated activities of left and right PFCs/PFC and cingulate cortex (perceives threat from competitors)
Suggested activity	1. SWOT analysis of self 2. Seek and accept feedback (criticism) 3. Take time to digest and accept criticism 4. Discuss improvement of personality traits with trusted friends 5. When you feel diminished in your own assessment or overwhelmed by criticism and put downs, say to yourself 'I am enough' 6. Use a self-worth metre to rate your level occasionally
Introspective activity	1. Learn to reappraise failure as learning 2. Observe how you behave when you win 3. Zoom out and observe yourself (be a witness) and assess yourself 4. Catch yourself when inner criticism and disappointment begin to damage self-esteem

(continued)

(continued)

Competence to Be Exercised (G)	Optimism
Brain structures involved	Left PFC and right insula
Suggested activity	1. Use any setback or frustrating bottleneck situation and try to see the bright side or possibility hidden behind the roadblock. Write them down and create an action plan around gaining advantage from the situation. 2. Remind yourself about the glass being half-full and not half-empty. Ensure that you do not undermine what you have due to disappointment about what you do not have. This may not be your natural pattern of thought. But because it is a conscious task, it is trainable by repeated practice. 3. Get excited about imperfection: Appreciate what is imperfect in a creation and how it enhances the whole.
Introspective activity	1. Become aware of the change of mood brought on by the reappraisal. Ensure balance by remaining realistic. 2. Be aware of factors that are making you fearful in spite of focus on the possibilities. 3. Congratulate yourself for changing perspective and mood.
Competence to Be Exercised (H)	Authentic Presence
Brain structures involved	Left PFC, insula
Suggested activity	1. Practise applying full attention to task, sport, dance and music 2. Practise active listening 3. Engage in breathing consciously and varying the rate 4. Practise gratitude meditation 5. Practise compassion meditation 6. Practise mindfulness during movement, for example, yoga 7. Prevent distractions, set specified time for smartphone use/Internet use/photography 8. Spend time in natural surroundings without a camera

Competence to Be Exercised (H)	Authentic Presence
Introspective activity	1. Notice the reduction of distracting signal noise in the brain 2. Be in touch with your core values 3. Resonate with the presence of the person before you feel the connection

Source: Author

Tan Tan: Ho ho! You tried to make it look serious and technical by putting it in frames and tables, but it's all quite common, everyday things to do.

Me: So do them. We have taken most of the competences for granted. That's why we neglect the practice that sharpens them and remain unaware about deficiencies.

Tan Tan: But this made me feel stupid because I thought the meditation the monks try to teach us was silly. When I go back to the monastery today, I get serious.

Me: You really serious about training? Then don't wait for someone to lay it all out for you. Take what you can from life. Although life seems the same as always, we know a little more from studying the brain in its working state. Now let's apply and use the information.

Tan Tan: I get opportunities to feel angry at least 10 times each day.

Me: Great! You will soon be a pro at anger management! Then we will have to get comfortable at being ourselves and allowing others to see who we really are.

Tan Tan: The second part is a lot more difficult.

Me: When we present ourselves as who we are not, a lot of energy is used in keeping the charade going and a great deal of fear lurks, taking up precious space in the brain, of being found out as a pretender. Shedding the shield and mask can be a big relief. It is well worth getting past the apprehension of being seen for real.

Tan Tan: What will people think?

Me: People deserve to know their leader through and through. The meditation and attentive listening will give you *presence*, but the requirement is of 'authentic presence'. The fear you experience at the prospect of laying your vulnerabilities open for inspection, the apprehension about 'What people will think' and the danger of people using your weaknesses to reject your leadership are common anxieties of all humans. Deep in their gut they know how much courage it takes to be transparent. Believe me, they will respect you for your openness. The love and acceptance that they do give in that condition is true, and they will respect you for your courage. Would you like others to be open and transparent when they interact with you?

Tan Tan: Yes, of course!

Me: Their fear about 'Will I be acceptable along with my flaws' applies to each one of us, but we don't know how to begin to get past it. We learn from someone who has got past fear. When you are a leader, you set the example. Like the example of being cool with having some weaknesses. Observe the design of a Masai Village on the Wild Serengeti in Tanzania. The leader's hut is located outside the protective walls built to protect the tribe. Clearly, the protector is open to attack.

Tan Tan: And he is cool with that?

Me: He sets the example of courage.

Tan Tan: Aren't parents the ones who set examples?

Me: Parents are leaders, so are teachers.

> *A sign of a Good Leader is not how many followers you have,*
> *but how many Leaders you create.*
>
> —Mahatma Gandhi

Tan Tan: Aah! That makes everyone a leader. That's not cool! To be better than the rest I have to learn to make thundering speeches.

Me: The quality of a leader and greatness emerge from the values others can learn from observing their conduct. Although speeches are inspiring, their message falls through if the person making the speech lives differently from the spoken word. The mismatch makes observers lose respect and reject the leader, though they may keep the speech. From great leaders, we learn inclusiveness, generosity, compassion, courage, humility, perseverance....

Tan Tan: Wait, wait! I have a problem with 'generosity'. I'm getting really angry that though I share my snack with Vivek every day, he refused to share colour pens with me during the art exam. Then he has the nerve to ask to share my food again!

Me: Let's talk about generosity through a story.

Tan Tan: Yeah, I like stories.

Me: There is a mythological story about two princes. Prince Truly Generous and Prince Wannabe Generous are cousins and Wannabe is resentful of the regard the subjects have for Truly. Wannabe asks the Royal Mentor, 'Why he is not regarded at par with Truly in terms of generosity'. The Royal Mentor decides to organize a test. He drives out of town towards a hilly rural area with Wannabe. The mentor uses magic to turn two hillocks into gold. The rules of the test are that Wannabe must give away all the gold and keep nothing for himself. The gold will replenish itself in case the giver derives any form of benefit during the giving process. At the end of the day, all the gold must be given.

Wannabe says, 'I can do this, but it is getting dark and the gold is not seen well enough'. I will start the giving in the morning. Then he walks into the villages nearby and announces that he will be giving away gold, so people please come to the hillside at dawn with whatever you can bring to carry away the gold. At dawn, the prince took a shovel and began the task of piling the yellow stuff on to carts, barrels, drums, bags and trays, and the folks saluted the prince and happily took it away. But oh dear! The mounds grew back. He shovelled harder and harder, but close to sundown the mounds were just as high as when he started. Wiping the sweat from his body; Wannabe gave up.

Just then Truly Generous came by that way. The mentor flagged him down and told him about the experiment, and asked would he like to try? Truly amiably said, 'Sure, why not!' After listening to the rules, he loiters a little near the gold. Two people passing by stop to look at the gold mounds glinting in the setting sun. Truly greets them and chats for half a minute. Then he walks back to where the mentor and Wannabe are waiting. He says, 'I'm done. I gave the mounds to those two people. Now may I leave?'

Tan Tan: How cool is that! He didn't sweat a single drop.

Me: For an act to qualify as 'generous', you cannot expect to derive any benefit at all, except the joy of giving. If you give to get a return favour, to get popular or get people to look up to you, that taints the generosity.

Tan Tan: Uh oh—looks like total disqualification!

Me: Experiments show that humans are more generous when significant levels of oxytocin are in circulation.

Tan Tan: That's the friendly bonding hormone.

Me: The hormone of social connection, nurturing and loving behaviour. Like love, generosity needs to be unconditional.

Tan Tan: Does love feature in leadership?

Me: The word 'love' is used in all sorts of ways, as a noun (a universal value/virtue), a verb (I care), a condition as in 'being in love' (when there is a combined surge of serotonin, dopamine, oxytocin and spikes of endorphin). In leadership, the universal value and caring nature of love are salient components.

Tan Tan: [*Tearfully*] When Mom calls the monastery, she says, 'I love you Tan Tan'; I guess she means that she cares, but from far away how can she care?

Me: She means that she wants you to become everything that is possible for you to be, to shine bright with the actualization of all your potential. Do you wish that for yourself?

Tan Tan: [*Wiping his nose on his sleeve*] I wish that for you too. Does that mean I love you?

Me: [*Grinning*] Yes. I love you too, Tan Tan. We can as a leader invoke that wish for every person in the team. Wish that each member rises to full potential, removing every obstacle in her/ his path. Then we can expand the boundaries of that wish and bestow good wishes on larger groups. This is an exercise for the topmost conscious level of the brain.

Tan Tan: Exercise? What is it called?

Me: Compassion meditation. It has immense benefits on the health of brain tissue, and it increases the bulk of the most evolved parts of the human brain, increasing its own potential.

Tan Tan: Awesome! You're telling me that making a wish inside of my head can be an exercise for my brain.

Me: A nourishing exercise! Armed with the awareness of applicable neuroscience and a goal to develop qualities that inspire; humans of all ages can practise required attributes in the laboratory of everyday life and develop a lasting increase in brain tissue thickness and enduring reset of physiology to states of equanimity.

Tan Tan: When will I know that I am done with my training to be a leader?

Me: Story time!

Mahatwa–Kanksha (MK) was the name of the heir apparent of a group of industries. From an early age, he was schooled in leadership competencies in the very best and specialized institutes under the watchful guidance of his mentor Professor Vinamra (Professor V, hereafter). MK's father, the big-time industrialist, wanted the son to carry on the baton of leadership and to take the Kanksha Group to greater heights, and was pleased with the development of qualities such as humility, responsibility and perseverance he observed in the young man. He was pleased that he had picked Professor V as the guide to design the training of his son to lead his group of companies from its present recognition tag of a 'Good Place to Work' towards the level of a 'Great Place to Work'.

The father decided that the time had come to conclude the training and to introduce his heir to the corporate office. He urged

MK to ask Professor V what he would like as a befitting gift, acknowledging his guidance, and with that gift he planned to request the Professor to write a leadership-qualifying certificate for the boy.

Professor V lived in a middle-class colony built cooperatively by a group of like-minded friends. The industrialist hoped that he would ask for a bungalow in the better part of the town and perhaps a donation for his library. Instead, Professor V said to MK, 'If you want to do me a favour before I certify that your training is complete, then please rid my colony of mosquitoes'. MK was surprised. 'Is that all you want me to do?', he exclaimed! Yes, just make sure you don't use the terrible fog of pyrethrin spray, because me and my friends can't tolerate that and nor can our grandchildren.

For months MK and all the might of the Kanksha Group did all that was necessary to keep the colony free from mosquitoes, but the whining arthropods flew right back. At some times, the numbers were few, but Professor V wasn't satisfied with a mere reduction. Eventually, Father K and Mahatwa came over to Professor V's house to apologize and to ask for the certificate of completion of leadership training. Professor V smiled. 'I didn't say you can't begin your role at the corporate office', he said. 'Go ahead and start your work, but know that the work of polishing and strengthening leadership competencies is never complete.'

Tan Tan: Strange, I'm not happy to hear this story, but I do feel excited that I want to do a thing that never ends. Is it better to become a master or keep trying to get there?

Me: We don't become things, Tan Tan. We are defined by what we do. I am not a writer, but I write. When I stop doing, thinking and participating, that's when I 'become' vegetative.

Tan Tan: I can lead from today, and I don't need a certificate of qualification to start. That feels nice, right here right now! But I heard someone say, It's not what you do but how you are that makes you a leader. Is that a noun or adjective? Transparent, brave, dependable....

Me: Those are qualities a leader must develop and sustain. Once I asked a little girl, 'What she wants to be when she grows up?' She burst into tears. 'Do children turn into things?', she asked between sobs. That really got me thinking. She already knew that becoming a thing is a punishment, as Oscar Wilde put it, 'You can be imprisoned if you think of yourself as a noun'. Go ahead and lead, take responsibility, inspire, blaze a trail but remain free, adaptable and resilient.

Tan Tan: And in good humour!

> *I never stopped trying to be qualified for the job.*
> —Darwin E. Smith, CEO Kimberly Clark
> (named Level 5 leader in *Good to Great* by Jim Collins)

GLOSSARY

BRAIN LOBES AND CEREBELLUM

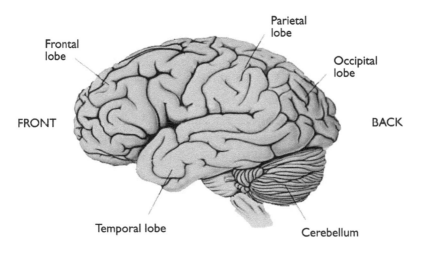

Adrenaline: Also known as adrenalin/epinephrine is a hormone
    secreted by the adrenal gland (medulla or core) and by neurons
    (nerve cells) in the brain. It is the chemical transmitter that
    mediates fear and prepares the body for 'fight or flee' response.
    It is also used as a medicine.
Altruism: Concern and action for the well-being and benefit of
    other humans and/or all creatures.

Amygdala: A part of the limbic system located in the mid-brain. An almond-shaped nucleus that plays a key role in the processing of emotions, especially fear, survival instinct and aggression.

Angular gyrus: A part of the parietal lobe of the brain that is close to the temporal lobe. This area participates in spatial awareness, attention, memory retrieval and out of body experience, apart from language and math.

Autonomic nervous system: A system of nerves that regulates the activity of organs such as heart, lungs, circulation and muscle responses to emotions and other physiological conditions, without conscious awareness.

Basal ganglia: Cell groups that lie deep within the brain substance that participates in motor control, motor learning (skill), executive functions and behaviour.

Brain map: Images produced by projecting functions (behaviour) on brain regions. Functional and structural neuro-imaging techniques are used to study and produce brain maps.

Brainstem: The central trunk of the mammalian brain consisting of the medulla oblongata, pons and mid-brain. It continues downwards to form the spinal cord.

Cerebellum: A part of the brain that is located at the back of the head, below the level of a cap. It coordinates voluntary movements such as posture, balance and speech, resulting in smooth and balanced muscular action.

Cingulate cortex: When the two halves of the brain are pulled apart, the cingulate cortex is seen just above the band (corpus callosum) that connects the two hemispheres. This arch-like tissue on both sides belong to the limbic system that participates in emotion and behaviour linked with motivation. It is also important in the process of learning and memory formation. The anterior cingulate cortex participates in the processing of pain.

Circadian rhythm: A biological clock. Changing body functions that follow a pattern linked with the time of day or night.

Cognition: Mental processes that occur with awareness, thinking, understanding, reasoning and knowing.

Depolarization: At rest, a typical nerve cell wall has electrical charge across the membrane. It is positively charged on the outside and negatively charged on its inside. When stimulated, a spot on the membrane loses its charge becoming less negative on the inside. This sets off a signal which flows through the length of the cell.

Dopamine: A neurotransmitter, one of the molecules that carry signals from one nerve cell to another. Dopamine is generally released from nerve ends in response to the perception of a reward.

Endocrine gland: Groups of cells that secrete hormones (chemical messengers) directly into the blood stream (without tubes/ducts) such as thyroid, adrenal, ovaries, testes and in the brain—pituitary, hypothalamus.

fMRI: A technique for scanning the brain while it is at work. It measures brain activity by detecting changes of blood flow to the area.

Forebrain: The part of the brain that evolved the latest, consists of the cerebrum, thalamus, hypothalamus and limbic system. It controls voluntary movement and the integration of sensory information to higher abstract thought, logic, speech and emotions.

Frontal lobe: Located just behind the forehead on both sides of the midline. This part of the brain is concerned with behaviour, learning, personality and movement.

Ganglion: Cluster of nerve cell bodies.

Hemispheres (brain): Two halves of the brain separated by the longitudinal fissure.

Hippocampus: A curved structure within the brain, a part of the limbic system that is involved in the formation of new memories and learning. There is one on each side.

Homeostasis: Tendency to return to equilibrium among interdependent processes.

Hypothalamo-pituitary-adrenal axis (HPA axis): A central stress-response system that interlinks the brain/nervous system and endocrine/hormone system to prepare the body to cope with conditions that threaten survival and well-being.

Inferior frontal gyrus: Lower part of the frontal lobe of the brain, just above the temporal lobe.

Insula: A lobe of the brain that is tucked behind the temporal lobe. It has functions such as subjective emotional experience, self-awareness, awareness of body and viscera (interoception), empathy and compassion.

Interoception: Sense of the internal state of body, awareness of breathing, heartbeat, tightness of muscles, relaxed and comfortable condition.

Kinesthesia: Awareness of the position and movement of the parts of the body by means of sensory organs (proprioceptors) in the muscles and joints.

Lateral ventricle: Cavity within each hemisphere of the brain containing cerebrospinal fluid, communicating with a system of smaller ventricles and ducts as well as the space around the brain enveloped by membranes called meninges.

Limbic system: A set of brain structures located below the cerebrum on both sides of the thalamus. It includes amygdala, hippocampus, nucleus accumbens, cingulate cortex—all participate in the generation of emotions, motivation, behaviour and memory. The limbic system is also called the paleomammalian cortex as it is evolved earlier than the thinking and reasoning neocortex.

Melanopsin: Light sensitive pigment found in the retina (innermost layer of the eye).

Mid-brain: The part of the brain that lies below the thalamus and connects to the brainstem. Also called 'mesencephalon' it processes visual and auditory data, generates reflex motor responses and participates in the maintenance of consciousness.

Mirror neuron: Motor neurons that fire when an individual performs an action and also fire when an individual merely observes another performing the same action. These are the basic units of learning by watching/mimicry and facilitators of empathy (feel how another maybe feeling).

Myelin: Protein-phospholipid sheath for nerve fibres that insulate and speed up nerve signal conduction.

Neural substrate: The nerve system or pathways that underlie a certain behaviour or psychological state.

Neuroleadership: Use of neuroscientific knowledge in areas of leadership development, management training, change management, education, consulting and coaching.

Neuron: Cell specialized to transmit impulses/nerve cell.

Neuroplasticity: Ability of the brain to form and reorganize synaptic connections to change and develop throughout life in response to experience, learning or injury.

Neurotransmitter: A chemical substance released at a nerve ending as a result of the arrival of an impulse. This diffuses across the synaptic cleft and is capable of generating a fresh impulse in the next nerve cell.

Ninja: Person trained in ancient Japanese martial art (Ninjutsu), especially skilled in stealth, camouflage and effective covert action.

Nociceptor: The sensory neuron that responds to painful and potentially damaging stimuli, for example, heat, and sends alarm signals to the spinal cord.

Nucleus accumbens: The part of the brain located in the basal forebrain and a part of the basal ganglia. It connects with the limbic system (mesolimbic pathway) and is stimulated during rewarding experiences. Nucleus accumbens is a brain structure that participates in forming memories involving salient environmental stimuli, both positive and negative.

Orbito-frontal cortex: The part of the frontal brain that sits above the eye sockets, is thought to participate in impulse control and response inhibition as well as in decision-making.

Oxytocin: A hormone and a neurotransmitter produced in the hypothalamus in response to hugging, touching and intimate activity. It is involved in social bonding, trust generation and generosity. As a hormone, it is required for regulating childbirth and breastfeeding. It also helps to reduce stress.

Pituitary gland: An organ at the base of the brain, about the size of a pea, known as the 'master gland' as it secretes many hormones, directs other glands to work, thus has profound effects all over the body.

Pre-frontal cortex: The anterior most part of the frontal lobes, highly developed in humans and participates in complex cognitive, emotional and behavioural functions.

Receptor: A molecule in a cell membrane which responds specifically to a particular neurotransmitter, hormone, antigen or drug.

Repolarization: Just after the depolarization of membrane potential by a passing stimulus, the membrane returns to a state of resting potential with higher negative charge on the inside of the membrane. The process takes a few milliseconds.

Retina: The nerve layer at the back of the eyeball that contains cells sensitive to light, which trigger nerve impulses that pass via the optic nerve to the brain where a visual image is formed.

Serotonin: A neurotransmitter also known as 5-HT and as 'happy hormone' as it gives a feeling of well-being. It is secreted in the brain, bowel and in blood platelets (as a constrictor of blood vessels).

Suprachiasmatic nucleus: A part of the hypothalamus located just above the crossing of the optic nerves. It regulates the body clock (circadian rhythm).

Temporal lobe: One of the major lobes of the brain located above the ear on both sides. It has many functions such as processing of language, emotional response, perception of sound, speech, memory and face recognition.

Viscera: Internal organs, for example, intestines, heart and liver.

BIBLIOGRAPHY

Babad, E. Y., J. Inbar, and R. Rosenthal. 'Pygmalion, Galatea, and the Golem: Investigations of biased and unbiased teachers.' *Journal of Educational Psychology* 74 (1982): 459–474.

Bartal, I., J. Decety and P. Mason. 'Empathy and Pro-Social Behavior in Rats.' *Science* 334, no. 6061 (2011): 1427–30.

Bartolo, A., F. Benuzzi, L. Nocetti, P. Baraldi, and P. Nichelli. 'Humor Comprehension and Appreciation an FMRI study.' *Journal of Cognitive Neuroscience* 18, no. 11 (2006): 1789–98.

Berk, L. S., S. A. Tan, W. F. Fry, B. J. Napier, J. W. Lee, R. W. Hubbard, J. E. Lewis, and W. C. Eby. 'Neuroendocrine and Stress Hormone Changes during Mirthful Laughter.' *American Journal of Medical Science* 298, no. 6 (1989): 390–96.

Bernhardt, Boris C., Tania Singer. 'The Neural Basis of Empathy.' *Annual Review of Neuroscience* 35 (2012): 1–23.

Blanke, Olaf. 'Out of Body Experience and Autoscopy of Neurological Origin.' *Brain* 127, no. 2 (2004): 243–58.

Bowen, Will. *A Complaint Free World: How to Stop Complaining and Start Enjoying the Life You Always Wanted.* New York, NY: Bantam Doubleday Dell Publishing Group, 2007.

Brosnan, Sarah F., and Frans B. M. de Waal. 'Monkeys Reject Unequal Pay.' *Nature* 425 (2003): 297–99.

Brown, Brene. *Daring Greatly.* New York, NY: Gotham, 2012.

Cardarelli Kathryn M., Sally W. Vernon, Elizabeth R. Baumler, Susan Tortolero, and David M. Low. 'Sense of Control and Diabetes Mellitus among US adults: A Cross-Sectional Analysis.' *Biopsychosocial Medicine* 1, no. 1 (2007): 19. doi 10.1186/1751-0759-1-19

Cardarelli, Roberto, Sandy-Asari Hogan, Kimberly G. Fulda, and Joan Carroll. 'The Relationship between Perceived Sense of Control and Visceral Adipose Tissue –North Texas Healthy Heart Study.' *BioPsychosocial Medicine* 5 (2011):12. doi:10.1186/1751-0759-5-12

Chang, E. C., and L. J. Sanna. 'Affectivity and Psychological Adjustment Across Two Adult Generations: Does Pessimistic Explanatory Style Still Matter?' *Personality and Individual Differences* 43 (2007): 1149–1159

Changeux, Jean-Pierre P., Antonio Damasio, and Wolf Singer, eds. *Neurobiology of Human Values*. Berlin: Springer, 2005.

Collins, Jim. *Good to Great*. New York, NY: Random House, 2001.

Craig, A. D. 'Interoception: The Sense of the Physiological Condition of the Body.' *Current Opinion in Neurobiology*, 13 (2003): 500–505.

Damasio, Antonio R. *Descartes Error: Emotion, Reason and the Human Brain*. New York, NY: Penguin Books, 1994.

———. *Self Comes to Mind: Constructing the Conscious Brain*. London: Vintage, 2012.

Davidson R. J., J. Kabat-Zinn, J. Schumacher, M. Rosenkranz, D. Muller, and S. F. Santorelli, et al. 'Alterations in Brain and Immune Function Produced by Mindfulness Meditation.' *Psychosomatic Medicine* 65, no. 4 (2003): 564–570.

Di Pellegrino, G., L. Fadiga, L. Fogassi, V. Gallese, and G. Rizzolatti. 'Understanding Motor Events: A Neurophysiological Study.' *Experimental Brain Research* 91 (1992): 176–80.

Doidge, Norman. *The Brain that Changes Itself: Stories of Personal Triumph from the Frontiers of Brain Science*. New York, NY: Penguin, 2008.

Eisenberger, Naomi I. 'The Pain of Social Disconnection: Examining the Shared Neural Underpinnings of Physical and Social Pain.' *Nature Reviews Neuroscience* 13 (2012): 421–434.

Goleman, Daniel. *Emotional Intelligence*. New York, NY: Bantam, 1995.

———. *Working with Emotional Intelligence*. New York, NY: Bantam, 1998.

———. *Social Intelligence*. New York, NY: Bantam, 2006.

Goleman, Daniel, Richard Boyatzis, and Annie McKee. *The New Leaders: Transforming the Art of Leadership into the Science of Results*. New York, NY: Time Warner Paperbacks, 2003.

Grassian, Stuart. 'Psychiatric Effects of Solitary Confinement.' *Journal of Law and Policy*, 22 no. 325 (2006): 325–383. http://openscholarship. wustl.edu/law_journal_law_policy/vol22/iss1/24

Harrington, D. L., L. A. Boyd, A. R. Mayer, D. M. Sheltraw, and R. R. Lee. 'Formulating Representations of Time: An Event-related fMRI Study.' *Proceedings of the International Cognitive Neuroscience Society* 1 (2002): 432–437.

Hojat, Mohammadreza, Michael J. Vergare, Kaye Maxwell, George Brainard, Steven K. Herrine, Gerald A. Isenberg, Jon Veloski, and Joseph S. Gonnella. 'The Devil is in the Third Year: A Longitudinal Study of Erosion of Empathy in Medical School.' *Academic Medicine* 84, no. 9 (2009): 1182–1191.

Kaye, Lenard W., and Clifford M. Singer, eds. *Social Isolation of Older Adults: Strategies to Bolster Health and Well-Being*. New York, NY: Springer Publishing Company, 2018.

Lovero, Kathryn L., Alan N. Simmons, Jennifer L. Aron, Martin P. Paulus. 'Anterior Insular Cortex Anticipates Impending Stimulus Significance.' *Neuroimage* 45, no. 3 (2009): 976–983.

Makinodan, Manabu, Kenneth M. Rosen, Susumu Ito, and Gabriel Corfas. 'A Critical Period for Social Experience Dependent Oligodendrocyte Maturation and Myelination.' *Science* 337, no. 6100 (2012): 1357–60.

Marcum, David, and Steven Smith. *Egonomics*. London: Simon and Schuster, 2008.

Pink, Daniel. *Drive: The Surprising Truth about what Motivates Us*. Edinburgh, Great Britain: Canongate Books, 2011.

Ramachandran, Vilayanur S. *The Emerging Mind*. London, UK: Profile Books with BBC, 2004.

———. *Tell Tale Brain*. London, UK: Random House, 2010.

Rosenthal, Robert, and Lenore Jacobson. *Pygmalion in the Classroom*. Norwalk, CT: Crown House Publishing, 1968.

Rowe, James B., Doris Eckstein, Todd Braver, and Adrienne M. Owen. 'How does Reward Expectation Influence Cognition in the Human Brain.' *Journal of Cognitive Neuroscience* 20, no. 11 (2008): 1–13.

Schmidt, Marco F. H., and Jessica A. Sommerville. 'Fairness Expectations and Altruistic Sharing in 15-Month-Old Human Infants.' *PLOS One* 6, no. 10 (2011): e23223. doi 10.137/journal.pone.0023223

Scott, D. J., C. S. Stohler, C. M. Egnatuk, H. Wang, R. A. Koeppe, and J. K. Zubieta. 'Individual differences in reward responding Explain Placebo Induced Expectations and Effects.' *Neuron* 55, no. 2 (2007): 325–336.

Seligman, Martin. *Learned Optimism.* New York, NY: Pocket Books, 1998.

Sen, Anjana. *Get the Ego Advantage!* New Delhi: SAGE Publications, 2006.

Shammi, P., and D. T. Stuss. 'Humor Appreciation: A Role of Right Frontal Lobe.' *Brain* 122, no. 4 (1999): 657–666.

Sharot, Tali. *Optimism Bias: A Tour of the Irrationally Positive Brain.* New York, NY: Pantheon, 2011.

Zahn, Roland, Jorge Moll, Mirella Paiva, Griselda Garrido, Frank Krueger, Edward D. Huey, and Jordan Grafman. 'The Neural Basis of Human Social Values: Evidence from Functional MRI.' *Cereb Cortex* 19 no. 2 (February 2009): 276–283 (Published online 2008 May 22; PMCID: PMC2733324). doi: 10.1093/cercor/bhn080

Zald, David H., and Scott Rauch. *Orbitofrontal Cortex.* New York, NY: Oxford University Press, 2006.

ABOUT THE AUTHOR

Consultant and coach for emotional intelligence and neuro-leadership since 2004, Dr Anjana Sen has authored a number of books, papers and book chapters. An alumnus of Lady Hardinge Medical College, New Delhi, Dr Sen was employed in the medical services of Oil and Natural Gas Corporation between 1985 and 2004. Her first book *Get the Ego Advantage!* was published in 2006 (SAGE). An illustrated screenplay *Adventure Ahead: The Inside Story* was published in 2018.

Her contribution is internationally recognized in the area of neurology of emotions, by the international professional body Consortium for Research on Emotional Intelligence in Organizations. Dr Sen was one of the founder members of the Forum for Emotional Intelligence Learning, which was founded in 2009 in Mumbai.

She designs and facilitates workshops on ego awareness and balance, stress management, relationship management, empathy enhancement and neuroleadership. She has served many corporate clients, speaks regularly at medical and management colleges and conferences in India and abroad. She also provides life coaching service based in New Delhi.

CPSIA information can be obtained
at www.ICGtesting.com
Printed in the USA
FFHW020815301219
57297664-62804FF